THINK HISTORY

MODERN TIMES
1750–1990

Susan Willoughby

Series editor: Lindsay von Elbing

FOUNDATION

heinemann.co.uk

✓ Free online support
✓ Useful weblinks
✓ 24 hour online ordering

01865 888080

Heinemann

Inspiring generations

Heinemann Educational Publishers
Halley Court, Jordan Hill, Oxford, OX2 8EJ
Part of Harcourt Education

Heinemann is the registered trademark of
Harcourt Education Limited

First published 2004

09 08 07 06 05 04
10 9 8 7 6 5 4 3 2 1

British Library Cataloguing in Publication Data is available from the British Library on request.

ISBN 0 435 31371 1

Designed, illustrated and typeset by IFA Design Ltd, Plymouth, Devon
Printed in Spain by Edelvives

Photographic acknowledgements
The author and publisher would like to thank the following for permission to reproduce photographs:
AKG, pages 141 (left), 157 (right) 158 (left and right); AP Photo, pages 101 (right), 103, 190 (right); Art Archive, pages 17, 22, 23 (bottom), 176, 213 (top); Associated Press, page 105; Bilderdienst Suddeutscher Verlag, page 129 (top); Bodleian Library, page 119; Bridgeman/ Manchester City Art Galleries, page 64; Commonwealth War Grave Commission, page 114; Corbis, pages 104, 108, 148 (bottom right); Corbis/Bettman, page 100; Corbis/Harcourt Index, page 148 (bottom left); Corbis/Richard T. Nowitz, page 145 (right); Deutsches Historisches Museum Berlin, page 126 (left); Fotomas Index, pages 29; Freemantle Media, page 45; Hulton Archive, pages 7 (bottom), 15, 21, 23 (top), 24 (top and bottom), 30, 42, 52, 57, 71, (top), 79 (top right, bottom left), 85, 89, 93 (top), 99 (top and bottom), 111, 118, 120 (bottom), 152, 204, 206 (top and bottom), 207 (top and bottom), 216 (right); Ronald Grant Archive, page 145, (top left); Illustrated London News, page 179; Imperial War Museum, pages 192 (left and middle), 196; Katz Pictures, page 209 (left); Mansell Collection, page 48; Mary Evans Picture Library, pages 4, 7 (top), 27, 53, 71 (bottom), 79 (middle, bottom right), 120 (top) 138, 157, (left), 214; PA Photos, page 218; Peter Newark's American Pictures, pages 79 (top left), 88, 93 (bottom), 102, 192 (right); Popperfoto, pages 144, 208, 209 (right); Public Record Office Image Library, pages 203 (top and bottom right), 216 (left); Punch, pages 5, 20, 73, 170; Schomburg Center for Research in Black Culture, New York, page 98; Science and Society, page 43; The Sternberg Centre, page 145 (bottom left); Topham Picturepoint, pages 74, 75, 101 (left), 141 (right), 177; University of Kent Centre for the Study of Cartoons and Caricatures, pages 189, 190 (bottom left); USHMM, courtesy of R. Harrison, page 142; USHMM Photo Archives, page 126 (right); Weiner Archive, pages 135, 140; Zydowski Institute, page 134; Source unknown, pages 55, 129 (bottom), page 148 (top), 163, 167, 190 (top left), 195, 201 (both), 213 (bottom), 215.

Cover photograph: 'Search lights in the night sky' from the Occupation Triptych, 1990, by Derek Crow, © the Bridgeman Art Library/Jersey Museum

Picture research by Frances Topp

Written source acknowledgements
The publishers have made every effort to contact copyright holders of material reproduced in this book. Any omissions will be rectified in subsequent printings if notice is given to the publisher. In some sentences the wording or sentence structure has been simplified.

CONTENTS

THEME: REVOLUTIONS

INTRODUCTION

WAS 1750 TO 1900 AN ERA OF PROGRESS?

In your study of History so far you may have learned about political revolutions – in England, France and America. This chapter is also about revolutions – but these are revolutions that had an impact on the everyday life of people and on Britain's wealth.

On 1 May 1851, the Great Exhibition was opened in London by Queen Victoria. It brought together thousands of exhibits. More than half of them were British. Approximately six million visitors came – many of them ordinary workers. The aim was to celebrate the progress being made in science, the arts and technology. The exhibition was also intended to show everyone that Britain was the leading industrial nation – the 'workshop of the world'. The organisers, including Prince Albert (Queen Victoria's husband), felt that Britain had made great progress in the nineteenth century. But did everyone feel the same way? Look at Sources A and B, which are about the Great Exhibition.

SOURCE (A)

A contemporary engraving showing some of the exhibits at the Great Exhibition in 1851.

A Punch cartoon from 1852 showing specimens from Mr Punch's industrial exhibition of 1850.

What different impressions of the Great Exhibition do you think are given by Sources A and B?

Why do you think the artists wanted to create this impression? Share your ideas with the rest of the class.

This was certainly an age of great change, but was it an age of progress? You will decide as you work through this section.

1 WERE THE CHANGES IN AGRICULTURE A REVOLUTION?

WHAT CHANGES TOOK PLACE IN FARMING AFTER 1700?

Objectives

In this section you will find out:
- how land was enclosed after 1700
- why land was enclosed after 1700.

To investigate these ideas you will:
- study a range of sources that outline the two systems of farming
- write a speech about the advantages or disadvantages of land enclosure.

Starter

Take a look at the bar chart and Sources A to D. Then brainstorm the questions that follow.

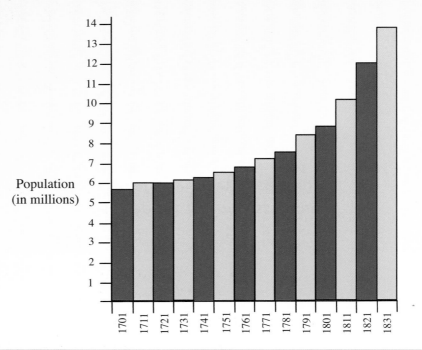

Bar chart showing the rising population in Britain, 1700–1830.

A contemporary view of the city of Manchester in 1850.

A contemporary picture showing farming in the nineteenth century.

One man has an acre of land divided into eight strips. The strips are spread over a large common field.

A description of farming methods in 1794.

Key words

Infectious A disease or illness that spreads easily and quickly.

If any animal had an **infectious** disease, nothing could stop it spreading through the flock.

From a report on farming in 1794.

💡 *Why do you think the demand for food increased in the nineteenth century?*

💡 *What clues can you find here that the old method of farming could not meet this demand? Share your ideas with the rest of the class.*

What was farming like in 1700?

In 1700 farming methods in England had not changed since the Middle Ages. Villages were surrounded by three large, unfenced, fields divided into many narrow strips. Each farmer owned or rented a number of strips scattered across the three fields. Sometimes these were two or three miles apart. The rich farmers decided which crops would be grown in the fields. These crops rotated each year around the three fields.

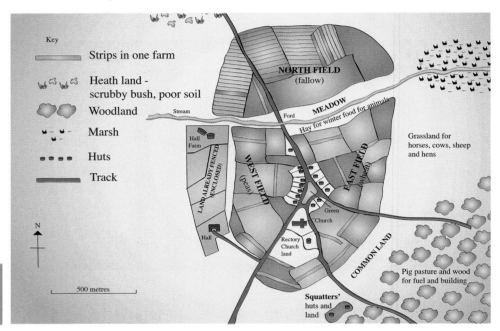

The open-field system of farming.

Three course rotation

Each year, two fields were sown with crops. The third was left **fallow**. Animals grazed on the stubble and weeds. Their manure fertilised the soil.

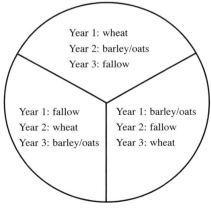

All the villagers had the right to graze their animals on the **common land** and to take timber from the woodland.

💡 Why do you think the three-course system was inefficient and unfair?

Key words

Fallow Land left empty of crops for a period of time.
Common land Land that all the villagers could use.
Squatter Someone who lives on an area of public land with no legal right to it.

What main changes took place in farming after 1700?

After 1700, farming had to change to feed the growing population. To improve production, farmers needed large blocks of land. So the small strips were put together to form large fields with hedges or fences around them. This process was called 'enclosure'. Most of the common land was also enclosed. People lost the right to cut timber in the woodland.

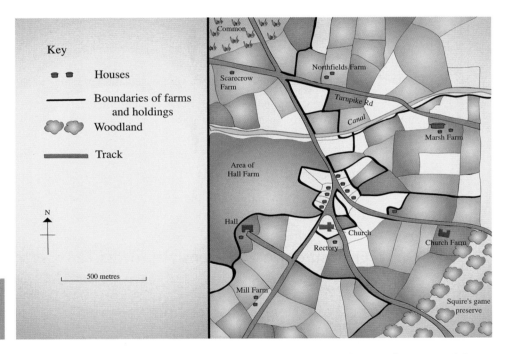

The village after enclosure.

Enclosure made some farmers richer than others. They could grow better crops in enclosed fields. From 1750, enclosure became very popular. By the middle of the nineteenth century, almost all the open fields had disappeared.

How was land enclosed?

Farmers who wanted to enclose their land had to get an Act of Parliament to make this happen. By law, if those farmers who together owned 80 per cent of the land agreed to enclosure then they could force it on all the rest.

An enclosure notice was put on the door of the village church.

Parliament was asked to pass an Enclosure Act for the village.

Commissioners (government officials) were sent to the village to survey the open fields. Villagers had to prove how much land they owned so that they could claim their share.

The land was divided into blocks. Farmers were given the land they were entitled to. Some people got better land than others.

Each farmer had to hedge or fence his land. If his land was away from the village, he built a farm house on his plot and a road leading to it.

Enclosure was an expensive process. Farmers had to:

- pay legal fees
- pay for hedging or fencing.

Small landowners soon found themselves in debt. They had to sell their plots to richer farmers.

The enclosure of land – good or bad?

TASKS...

1 Below is a list of statements. Some support enclosure and some oppose it.

On a chart like the one below, write the numbers of the statements that support enclosure. Then write the numbers of the statements that oppose it. **WS**

Statements that support enclosure	Statements that oppose enclosure

1 *We all have a fair share of good and bad land.*

2 We waste too much time travelling between our strips. We need large fields close together.

3 We cannot use the new tools such as the seed drill because our strips are too small.

4 We support ourselves – we grow our own food and rear our own livestock.

5 *Weeds from strips belonging to lazy farmers spread to our land.*

6 We are free to experiment with new methods to increase our **yield**.

7 *Enclosure is expensive. Not everyone will be able to afford to pay for new fences, farmhouses and roads.*

8 We can breed healthier animals that produce more milk and better meat.

9 *We will lose our right to cut timber from the woodland and graze our animals on the common land.*

10 We will have more land, because the common land, meadows, woodland and wasteland will be shared out.

11 There will be more poverty in the village. More people will be landless. There will be fewer jobs for them.

12 *Too much land is left uncultivated each year. This is wasted.*

Key words

Yield The amount produced.

TASKS...

1 Imagine it is 1700. You and the other villagers are holding a meeting to decide whether all the open fields should be enclosed.

   a) Look at the two sides of the argument presented by the **freeholder** and the **yeoman**.

I have four strips of land scattered over three main fields. Two of my strips are on poor land so they do not produce much food. To make ends meet, I keep geese and chickens on the common. Enclosing the land in the village would mean paying legal fees and building fences. I could not afford all this. I no longer have the documents to prove that I own the land I farm.

A poor freeholder.

*I have twelve strips of land scattered over three fields. I know there is money to be made in the new farming methods. I want to grow vegetables instead of wheat and barley. However, not everyone in the village agrees with my decision. I want to try **selective breeding**, but there is no point because I cannot separate my animals from other animals on the common.*

A wealthy yeoman.

   b) Now use the statements you sorted on page 11 to complete a speech for *either* the freeholder *or* the yeoman. You need to persuade people to agree with your view about enclosure.

   Guidelines are provided on the next page to help you write the speech. **WS**

Key words

Freeholder Someone who owned or rented a small amount of land in the village.
Yeoman Someone who was a wealthy landowner.
Selective breeding Choosing only the best animals to breed from.

TASKS...

Tips for writing your speech

- Open with a strong statement saying why you think your view should be chosen.
- Give each of the reasons for your view. Explain these carefully.
- Explain why the opposite view should not be accepted.
- End your speech by briefly bringing together your main arguments.
- Write your speech in the first person and the present tense.
- Try to use connecting words such as *in fact, because, therefore, however*.
- Use words that will influence others in the village such as *obviously, surely, undoubtedly*.

Plenary

Study the following charts about the village of Aldsworth in Gloucestershire.

	Before enclosure	After enclosure
Land sown with wheat	200 **acres**	390 acres
Land sown with barley	200 acres	390 acres
Land sown with oats and peas	300 acres	390 acres
Total land cultivated	700 acres	1170 acres
Sheep bred each year	200	1800

	Before enclosure	After enclosure
Wheat	150 **quarters**	585 quarters
Barley	250 quarters	825 quarters
Amount of oats and peas produced	320 quarters	950 quarters
Total amount of crops grown	720 quarters	2360 quarters
Number of fleeces per **tod**	8	5

Key words

Acre A measure of land (about 4 kilometres square).
Quarter A grain measure of 8 bushels (about 13 kilograms).
Tod A weight of wool (about 13 kilograms).

- What were the main results of enclosure for Aldsworth?
- How would landowners benefit from enclosure?
- How would the people in towns and cities benefit from enclosure?

Discuss your answers with others in your class.

WHAT WERE THE EFFECTS OF ENCLOSURE?

Objectives

In this section you will find out:
- how enclosures led to other changes in farming methods in the eighteenth and nineteenth centuries
- the effects of those changes.

To investigate these ideas you will:
- complete diagrams of different types of crop rotation
- draw a graph using source material.

Starter

Take a look at Source A.

1771: In the **vale** of Evesham, the average fleece is 9 pounds (4 kilograms) from enclosed land, but only 3 pounds (1.35 kilograms) in the open fields. By enclosing, one sheep gives as much fleece as three used to.

1774: Where land is enclosed, several men work all winter hedging and ditching. In the open field system, where half or a third of the land is left empty, there is no work.

1801: Mr Foster (a commissioner) told me that, in 19 of the 20 Enclosure Acts that he had been responsible for, 2000 people had suffered as a result. He felt sad and partly responsible for the twenty families in each parish who had been made poorer by the Act. The poor in these parishes may say, and with truth, 'All I know is I had a cow, and an Act of Parliament has taken it from me.'

1813: From Lincoln to Barton, almost all of the land was **heath**, but now it is enclosed by Acts of Parliament. The result has been that the **tenants** live much better.

The records of a farmer, Arthur Young, from 1771 to 1813.

💡 *What is Arthur Young saying about the advantages and disadvantages of enclosure?*

💡 *Can you think of any reasons why Arthur Young could say such different things about the effects of enclosure? Discuss these reasons with other people in your class.*

How did enclosures lead to an increase in agricultural production?

Once land had been enclosed, some farmers were able to experiment with new machinery, crops, methods of cultivation, fertilisers and selective breeding. These new methods led to an increase in agricultural production.

New machines

In 1701 Jethro Tull invented the seed drill. This sowed seeds in straight rows and covered them up with earth afterwards. Before this, seeds had been sown by hand. The enclosure of farmland led to the seed drill being more widely used in the nineteenth century.

A painting from 1720 of the inventor, Jethro Tull.

💡 Why do you think that enclosure led to the seed drill being more widely used?

Ploughs were also improved:

- the Rotherham plough invented in 1760 needed fewer horses to pull it
- an all-iron plough was developed in the early 1800s
- in 1826 the first steam plough was developed.

In 1786, the **threshing** machine was invented; its use became more common in the 1820s.

💡 What effect do you think these new machines had on farm labourers?

Key words

Threshing Separating the wheat from the stalks it grows on.

New methods of cultivation

The four field system of crop rotation improved production in arable (crop growing) areas. This system was developed by Viscount Townshend, a landowner in Norfolk. Townshend grew barley, wheat, turnips and clover in rotation.

This new rotation system increased crop yields (the amount produced) because:

- clover and turnips put the goodness back into the soil
- there was no need to leave land uncultivated.

Animals grazed on the fields of clover. As they ate, they added manure to the soil. Turnips and clover provided **fodder** that could be stored and then fed to animals in winter. This meant that animals no longer had to be slaughtered in autumn.

TASKS...

1 a) Copy these two diagrams into your exercise book.

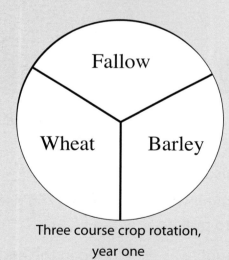

Three course crop rotation,
year one

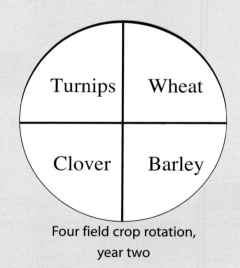

Four field crop rotation,
year two

b) Work out which crops would be grown in each field in years 2, 3 and 4.

2 What do you think were the benefits of the four field crop rotation system? Explain your answer carefully.

New fertilisers

Fertilisers enrich the soil and increase crop yields. Animal manure was the easiest fertiliser to use. From the 1840s, artificial fertilisers made from chemicals were also available.

After enclosure, some farmers used a method called marling to improve the quality of soil for growing crops. This involved adding:

- chalk or lime to heavy clay soils
- clay to light soils.

Selective breeding

After enclosure, some farmers tried to improve the quality of sheep and cattle by using only the best animals for breeding. This process was called selective breeding. It was pioneered by Robert Bakewell, who became famous for his New Leicester sheep. The results of selective breeding can be seen in Source C and the table below.

SOURCE C

A contemporary painting showing the results of selective breeding in the nineteenth century.

	1710	**1790**
Cattle	370lbs (168kg)	800lbs (363kg)
Calves	50lbs (23kg)	143lbs (65kg)
Sheep	28lbs (13kg)	80lbs (36kg)
Lambs	18lbs (8kg)	50lbs (23kg)

Average weight of animals sold at Smithfield Market in London, 1710–90.

Was enclosure good for everybody?

As you already know, enclosure led to poverty and hardship for many villagers.

- Farmers lost their land if they could not provide legal documents to prove it was theirs.

- Those who did receive small plots of land could not afford the cost of enclosure and usually sold up to wealthier neighbours.

- Cottagers were very badly affected. They were the poorest people who had no land and depended on working for others. After enclosure, there was no work for them. Many were forced to leave their homes.

- Poorer villagers also lost the right to use the common land for their animals and to collect wood.

- Many labourers lost their jobs after enclosure because there was no need for so many workers. As a result, farm labourers went in search of work in the new factories in towns. They hoped to find better paid jobs and a better life.

TASKS...

1 Could enclosure have been done differently to reduce the poverty and hardship suffered by many villagers?

2 'The benefits of increased production were greater than the disadvantages of poverty for some villagers.' Do you agree or disagree with this view? Explain your answer.

Farming in the nineteenth century
The Corn Laws, 1815

Between 1793 and 1815, Britain was at war with France. During this period, food was in short supply because the French were able to stop cheap wheat reaching Britain from Europe. This was good news for British farmers who made large profits, because they could sell their wheat for high prices. This made bread expensive.

When the French Wars ended in 1815, cheaper foreign wheat came into Britain. Farmers knew that the price of their wheat would fall. They might even go out of business. Therefore, in 1815 they persuaded Parliament to pass the Corn Laws. This was easy because many rich landowners were also MPs. The Corn Laws protected farmers but kept bread prices high. They lasted until 1846.

After 1815, life became harder for farm labourers. High bread prices caused hardship and at the same time, the demand for farm labourers fell. Many faced unemployment and lower wages. As a result, they became desperate and occasionally violent. Angry farm labourers sometimes carried out acts of **sabotage** and **arson**. In 1830, there was an outbreak of rioting in the southern counties of England, known as the Swing Riots (see Chapter 3, pages 43, 44–5 and 46).

Key words

Sabotage The destruction of an employer's property by workers.
Arson The act of deliberately and illegally setting fire to something.

Many farm labourers left rural areas in search of work in the new factory towns. This changed the balance of the population between the towns and countryside. In 1801, 69 per cent of the population lived in the countryside. By 1881, this figure had fallen to 32 per cent.

TASKS...

The word 'revolution' describes events that bring about dramatic change. You must now decide: *Were the changes in agriculture a 'revolution'?* **WS**

Firstly draw two columns labelled 'Before' and 'After'. Sort all the points that you think answer this question under these two headings. You will need to say what things were like before and after the changes.

Begin by explaining that the changes in agriculture have been called a 'revolution'. Say briefly that you are to decide if this is an accurate description of what happened. Now use the points from your lists to help you explain your decision. Write in the third person. Try to use words like *however*, *for example*, *as a result* to link the points you make.

TASKS...

Try to find any points that suggest that agriculture just changed over time, that it was not a 'revolution'. In the next paragraph try to suggest the opposite view, giving your examples. You might begin by saying *On the other hand…*.

In your conclusion, decide what you think about the question. You could begin by writing, *After weighing up the information…*. Use words like *although, however, for example*, as you briefly sum up the reasons for your decision.

SOURCE D

A *Punch* cartoon of 1844 called 'The Home of the Hayrick-burner'.

Plenary

Take a look at Source D. What do you think the man in the cartoon is being encouraged to do?

What message do you think the artist wanted to give people about the hardship faced by farm labourers in the period after 1815? Explain your answer carefully.

2

WERE THE CHANGES IN INDUSTRY A REVOLUTION?

WHAT CHANGES TOOK PLACE IN THE COTTON TEXTILE INDUSTRY?

Objectives

In this section you will find out:
- the changes that took place in the cotton textile industry
- how these changes affected the production of cotton
- how machines changed the way people worked.

To investigate these ideas you will need to:
- work out how you think machines improved production
- decide how factory work changed people's lives.

Starter

Take a look at Sources A and B.

SOURCE Ⓐ

Spinning wool at home in the eighteenth century.

SOURCE Ⓑ

Sixty years ago, cotton mills did not exist. Now there are at least 65. These cotton spinning mills are all worked by steam power – there is a plentiful supply of coal in the area to provide fuel for the mills. The mills are also linked by good canals. Oldham is close to Manchester, the main market for selling cotton. All this has helped to make Oldham one of the largest areas of **manufacture** in the country.

A description of Oldham by Edward Baines, 1825.

💡 *What changes have taken place in the textile industry from Source A to Source B?*

💡 *According to Edward Baines, what has made these changes possible?*

Share your answers to these two questions with the rest of the class.

Key words

Manufacture When goods are produced by machinery on a large scale.

Key words

Industrial Revolution A period of great change after about 1770 when people began to make goods in factories using machines.

The **Industrial Revolution** changed many old industries in Britain and created new ones. To help you understand the changes that took place and the impact of those changes, the next section will take a closer look at just one – the cotton industry.

Inventions in the cotton industry

Demand for cotton cloth increased because the population was growing and cotton cloth was cheaper than wool. This meant that cloth had to be produced quickly and in larger quantities. New machines helped this to happen.

TASKS...

As you read through the following factfiles on inventions in the cotton textile industry, on pages 22–4, complete a chart like the one below. **WS**

Invention	Inventor	Date of invention	Advantages of invention	Disadvantages of invention
	John Kay	1733		
Spinning Jenny	James Hargreaves			
Water Frame		1769		
	Samuel Crompton	1779		
Power loom	Edmund Cartwright			

factfile 1

Invention: The Flying Shuttle
Date: 1733
Inventor: John Kay of Bury, Lancashire
Power source: Hand power

The Flying Shuttle speeded up weaving and produced more cloth. Only one weaver was now needed to weave on a broadloom instead of two. Some handloom weavers saw the Flying Shuttle as a threat to their jobs because fewer weavers were needed to make the same amount of cloth. Demand for cotton for weaving rose as a result.

SOURCE C

The Flying Shuttle.

factfile 2

Invention: The Spinning Jenny
Date: 1767
Inventor: James Hargreaves of Blackburn, Lancashire
Power source: Hand power

The Spinning Jenny could be used in people's homes. It enabled a spinner, or 'jenny', to produce eight times more **yarn** than on a spinning wheel. It made a fine but weak thread. Many spinners hated it because they thought it threatened their jobs. However, it meant that spinners could provide more yarn for weaving.

SOURCE D

A diagram from around 1750 showing the Spinning Jenny.

Key words

Yarn Thread.

factfile 3

Invention: The Water Frame
Date: 1769
Inventor: Richard Arkwright of Preston, Lancashire
Power source: Water/steam power

The Water Frame made a strong and tough yarn. This was coarse and not as fine as that made by the Spinning Jenny. It was operated by water or steam power, which meant that it could not be used in the home and needed to be put in a factory. The Water Frame made spinning a much quicker process than weaving.

SOURCE E

A modern photograph of the Water Frame.

factfile 4

Invention: The Spinning Mule
Date: 1779
Inventor: J. Samuel Crompton of Bolton, Lancashire
Power source: Water/steam power

The Spinning Mule spun cotton on to 48 **spindles** at once. The yarn it made was finer than that made on a Water Frame and stronger than the yarn made on a Spinning Jenny.

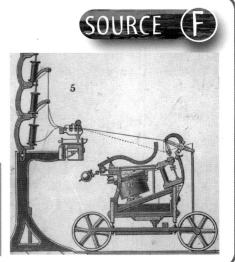

SOURCE F

A diagram from the time of the Spinning Mule.

factfile 5

Invention: The Power Loom
Date: 1785
Inventor: Edmund Cartwright, a vicar from Leicestershire
Power source: Water/steam power

Cartwright's Power Loom speeded up the weaving process. At first, it did not work well. Then two factory owners, William Horrocks and Richard Roberts, made some improvements to the design in the early 1800s. When the Power Loom came into use, mill owners could produce cloth of the same quality as handloom weavers but faster. By the 1820s, thousands of handloom weavers had lost their jobs.

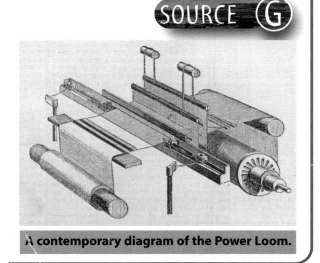

SOURCE G

A contemporary diagram of the Power Loom.

Year	Value of exports in £s
1710	5698
1751	45,986
1780	355,060
1800	5,406,501

Cotton exports, 1710–1800.

TASKS...

1 Carefully study the chart you filled in about the cotton inventions (see page 22).

   a) Now look at these two statements.

   All the cotton inventions were equally important because …

   The invention of …………………… *was more important than the rest because* …

   Choose the information from your chart to complete each of the statements. Try to explain in as much detail as possible.

   b) Compare your answers with the rest of the class. Which of these two statements do you agree with? Explain your decision.

2 It is 1851. The organisers of the Great Exhibition (see page 4) want to include the one most important invention that has mechanised the production of cotton. Write a letter to them saying which they should choose and why.

   ### Purpose of the letter

   To persuade people to agree with the invention of your choice.

   ### Letter lay out

   Your letter is going to important people. Include an address and date. Start it with *Dear Sirs* and end with *Yours faithfully*.

   ### What your letter should say

   Start with a strong statement about the invention you think should be chosen. Explain why you believe it has changed cotton production so much. Then say why the others should not be chosen.

   ### Word level

   You need to use words that will persuade the organisers to accept your choice such as *obviously, important, surely, undoubtedly*.

How did the new machines change the way people worked?

Read the views of the two historians below.

Before factories, families worked together in the home on simple hand-operated machinery. Children prepared the cotton for spinning, women spun yarn and men wove the yarn into cloth. They decided their own working hours. Most workers lived in the countryside in small, dark, damp cottages. Many cottages had only one room downstairs. In summer, these rooms were hot and airless.

Workers depended on the merchant for work. He fixed their rate of pay but only paid them for what they made. Many workers borrowed money from him to tide them over when there was no work or when prices were low.

Working in the mills was dangerous and unhealthy. Labourers worked a twelve hour day in hot, damp and humid conditions. Cotton dust choked their eyes and lungs. The noise of the machines was deafening. The machines had no safety guards so injuries were common.

Workers had to obey strict rules and suffered harsh punishments if they broke them – they were fined and sometimes beaten. Even seven-year-old children worked long hours. Many children became deformed from bending and crouching for long periods. Workers were beaten if they fell asleep or stopped working.

Factory workers earned at least 25 per cent more than farm workers. Women and children were mainly employed in the mills, where they could operate factory machinery. Because they were paid less than men were, there was less work for men in the spinning mills.

💡 Is Historian 1 suggesting that people were better off when they worked at home?

💡 Is Historian 2 saying that factory work was better or worse than farm work?

Explain your answers.

Plenary

Write down five things that you have learned about how the cotton industry changed. Share these with others in the class.

WERE FACTORIES REALLY THAT BAD?

Objectives

In this section you will find out:

- whether working conditions in all factories were bad.

To investigate these ideas you will:

- use sources to find out about working conditions for children
- look at what historians have said about these working conditions.

Starter

Look at Source A below. It was published in 1816, and it is by George Cruickshank, a famous cartoonist. When you study the cartoon, remember that most children did not go to school. It was expected that by seven years of age, children would be at work. This was not a new idea. Before factories existed, children helped their parents working in the fields and in the home.

SOURCE Ⓐ

A cartoon by George Cruickshank, commenting on the treatment of children working in factories.

- 💡 *What do you think is happening in this cartoon?*

- 💡 *What do you think the cartoonist is saying to us about working conditions for children?*

- 💡 *Do you think that Source A gives a true picture of working conditions for children? Why? What will help you to decide?*

To help us decide if Cruickshank is giving us a true picture of working conditions for children, we need to know more about him. Read the information below, which tells you more about the cartoonist.

- *George Cruickshank was against children working in factories.*
- *Robert Peel was the politician chairing a committee investigating working conditions in 1816.*
- *Robert Peel was also a mill owner with a reputation for treating his workers well.*
- *George Cruickshank probably never visited Robert Peel's mill.*

💡 *What do you think about the cartoon now that you know more about Cruickshank? You need to explain your thoughts.*

How did factory owners treat their workers?

When factories were first built, factory owners could make their own rules and regulations. They wanted to make a profit so they took advantage of their workers. They made them work long hours for little pay. Women and children were particularly badly treated. There were no laws to protect them from this.

Mill owners were keen to employ children as they could pay them very little. Children were also small enough to crawl under machines to clean them. Their small hands made them good 'piecers'. Their job was to join together broken threads while the spinning machines were still moving. Some children worked with their parents in the mills. Others were orphans from the cities who had become **apprentices**.

Overlookers, or overseers, were employed to make sure that children worked hard all day. These men were paid according to the amount of work that the children did.

Key words

Apprentice A young person who was taught a skill and given board and lodging by their employer.
Overlooker A person in charge of factory workers.

SOURCE B

This picture comes from the book *The Adventures of Michael Armstrong, Factory Boy* by Francis Trollope. The story is about an orphan boy who started work at the age of six and was mistreated. It is based on the real life story of Robert Blincoe.

SOURCE C

Once, two handles weighing a pound [0.5kg] each were screwed to my ears. Another time, three or four of us were hanged by our hands above the machinery. Sometimes we had to stand up in a skip without our shirts on, and we were beaten with straps. Overlookers used to tie a 28-pound [about 14kg] weight to us and this hung down our backs.

Written by Robert Blincoe in 1828. He was an orphan who worked in the mills from an early age. His work made him deformed.

SOURCE D

Question: Did working in the card-room affect your health?
Answer: Yes. It was so dusty. The dust got in my lungs and the work was so hard. I got so bad in health, that when I pulled the baskets down, I pulled my bones out of their places.

An interview with Elizabeth Bentley in 1832. She worked in the factories as a child.

Hundreds of accounts like those in Sources C and D were collected and used in reports about child labour. However, only the worst examples of cruelty were put in the reports, so they may not give a true picture of child labour. Some factory reformers told witnesses to describe only the worst things that had happened to them.

Seventeen years ago a group of us bought the New Lanark Mill [in Scotland]. There we found 500 children working thirteen hours a day. They were deformed and had stopped growing. They could not even learn the alphabet. I came to the conclusion that the children were injured by working in the mills so young and for such long hours.

Robert Owen, a mill owner, wrote this in 1816 to explain to Parliament why he did not employ children under the age of ten.

Question: Have you observed that children in the factories have particular accidents?
Answer: Children's hands and arms often get caught in the machinery. In many instances the muscles and the skin is stripped down to the bone. In some instances, a finger or two might be lost.

The observations of Dr Michael Ward in 1819.

From a book published in 1835. It was written by Edward Baines, a newspaper editor who defended mill owners and how they ran their mills.

It is said that children are so cruelly beaten by the overlookers that they become deformed and they grow up cripples. Some say children are forced to work thirteen, fourteen or fifteen hours per day. I think this is unusual. Children's work could not be easier! The children stand up straight, walk about, and often have the opportunity to sit down if they want to. The tiny fibres of cotton in the air are said, even by medical men, not to be harmful to young persons.

Written by Edward Baines in his newspaper, the Northern Mercury.

Key words

Corporal punishment To punish somebody by hitting or beating them.

I have visited many factories and I never saw **corporal punishment** of a child. The children seemed always to be cheerful and alert. They enjoy showing off how good they are at their work to any stranger. They showed no sign of being exhausted at the end of the day.

At Quarry Bank, near Wilmslow in Cheshire, there is a good-looking house. It was built as a home for the female apprentices. They are well fed, clothed and educated. The apprentices have milk-porridge for breakfast, potatoes and bacon for dinner, and meat on Sundays.

Written by Andrew Ure, a factory owner in 1835. Some employers like Ure believed that the factory system was good for workers.

At the Bradford factory of Mr John Wood, workers looked healthy. They work no more than eleven hours each day. A doctor is provided by the firm. If he notices anyone looking ill, he asks the reason and gives medicine if needed. Sick workers are sent home immediately. During the time they may be off work, they are paid their normal wages.

Written by William Dodd in 1841.

TASKS...

1 Read the text on page 28, then take a good look at Sources B to J before answering the following questions.
   a) Down one side of a page, make a list of the sources that oppose the use of child labour in factories and those that support child labour.
   b) At the side of each source, write down those words and phrases that each person uses to show what he or she thinks about the use of child labour in factories.
   c) Talk about the authors of these sources in pairs, in small groups or with your teacher. Which accounts, if any, do you believe? You must to be able to explain your viewpoint.
   d) Can you be sure that the children were so badly treated in all factories?
   e) What other kinds of evidence do you need?

TASKS...

2 Work in groups to complete one of the following tasks.

It is 1833. Parliament is to be asked to pass laws preventing factory owners from employing children. Some owners are claiming that this is not necessary. Decide in your group which of these campaigns you want to join:

- the campaign to stop child labour
- the campaign to support the factory owners' right to employ children.

If you choose the first option, you will need to include some of the worst examples of how badly some children were treated (look at Sources B to F).

If you choose the second, you will need examples that show how some factory owners treated their child workers well (look at Sources G to I).

Remember that your leaflet has to persuade people so think about the words and phrases you will need to use. You will also need a catchy slogan.

You can use the next points in both leaflets but the content will be different.

- Start by explaining who the children were and where they came from.
- Go on to describe how child workers are treated in factories.
- Finish off by making a strong statement to Parliament saying why you believe that child labour in factories should or should not be banned.

How well did you do?

Share your leaflet with other groups in the class. How does yours compare with theirs? Look at:

- the words you used to persuade your readers
- the examples you used to support your case.

Think about what you contributed to the work of the group.

Agree what you and your group might try to do better next time.

Were factory workers slaves?

Key words

Strap A leather belt used to beat children.

Thousands of people like ourselves – men, women and children – are now in a state of slavery. Every morning innocent children are driven to work crying with fear of the overlooker's **strap**. They hurry half-dressed to the woollen mills of Bradford. Thousands of little children from seven to fourteen years old forced to work every day from six in the morning to seven in the evening, with only 30 minutes for food and play. Poor infants!

A letter written by Richard Oastler to the Leeds Mercury. He wrote several letters in the 1830s under the heading of 'Yorkshire slavery'. He compared the working conditions of children in the mills to slavery in the British Empire.

In my recent tour of the factory districts, I have seen tens of thousands of people of all ages earning a good living in factories. They do their work without even getting hot, protected from the summer sun and winter frost, in bright, airy and healthy factory buildings. The power of steam has replaced the need for the hard labour of the workers.

Written by Andrew Ure, a factory owner, in 1835.

TASKS...

Carefully read Sources K and L.

1   What do you think Richard Oastler was trying to do by writing in the newspaper that factory workers were slaves?
2   Why do you think the writers have such different views about the use of child labour in textile mills? Explain your answer carefully.

Did working conditions improve?

At the start of the nineteenth century, the government believed that factory owners should be left to run their factories as they wished. However, by 1850 the government's attitude had changed. The activities of men like Robert Owen, Richard Oastler and Lord Shaftesbury persuaded Parliament to investigate working conditions in factories. The findings of these investigations resulted in the government passing laws to improve working conditions for men, women and children. The table on the next page gives details about the main laws that were passed in the nineteenth century.

1833	No children under the age of nine should work. Children aged between nine and thirteen could work no more than 48 hours a week. Children aged between thirteen and sixteen could work no more than 69 hours a week. Children must have two hours at school each day. Children under eighteen should not work at night. Four factory inspectors were appointed to ensure the law was enforced.
1844	Children under the age of eight were not allowed to work. Children aged between eight and thirteen were only allowed to work six and a half hours a day. Children under the age of eighteen and women should work no more than twelve hours a day. All dangerous machinery had to be fenced off.
1847	Women and children under the age of eighteen could work only ten hours a day.
1895	Children under the age of thirteen could work only 30 hours a week.

Some factory owners broke these laws.

💡 Which laws would be hardest to force factory owners to follow?

💡 Why do you think the factory owners broke the laws?

TASKS...

A revolution is a complete change. Do you think that industry went through a revolution during the nineteenth century? Explain your answer fully.

Plenary

Imagine a local museum is creating an exhibition about working conditions for children in the nineteenth century. Make a list of the sources you would include to make sure that visitors had a fair and balanced impression of factory work in the nineteenth century. Share your ideas with the rest of the class.

HOW DID THE RAILWAYS CHANGE BRITAIN?

Objectives

In this section you will find out:
- how and why railways developed
- how railways helped industry
- how railways improved people's leisure time.

To investigate these ideas you will:
- compare evidence to make judgements about early railway engines
- classify effects on a mind map.

Top speed, 100 mph.	Top speed, 125 mph.
London to Fishguard in five hours.	London to Fishguard in 4 hours 28 minutes.
Five carriages carrying up to 284 passengers; 42 first-class seats.	Five first-class carriages; one third-class carriage; one mail van; two dining carriages.
Driver and fireman on each engine; one guard at the back of the train and several attendants in dining carriages.	One driver; one train manager; two customer service hosts.
Buffet car with standing room only from London to Cardiff; trolley service on connecting train from Cardiff to Fishguard.	First-class dining with waiter service; full three-course meal available.
First-class return ticket, £157.	First-class return ticket, £56 to £197.

Starter

Look at the statements below. The facts and figures describe the train journey from London to Fishguard (which is in west Wales) in two different centuries. Then answer the questions that follow.

- *Which statements do you think describe the journey in 1900? Which describe the journey in 2002?*

- *Which journey do you think offers the most comfort and value for money?* **WS**

Facts and figures that describe the train journey from London to Fishguard in two different centuries.

The potential of railways

In the late eighteenth and nineteenth centuries methods of transport changed dramatically. People could travel around more easily on better roads. Goods could be carried on canals and rivers. But the most dramatic improvement came with the coming of the railways. They eventually made travel faster and more comfortable.

You know from the Starter exercise on page 35 how important railway travel has become. In this section you will find out how this revolution in transport came about.

Railways were not new. Simple, horse-drawn wagons had been used for some time in industries such as coal mining. They ran on tracks made first of wood and then iron. In the early nineteenth century, Richard Trevithick began to experiment with steam engines.

The Rainhill Trials

This was a competition to find a steam engine to pull a passenger train on the new Liverpool to Manchester railway. The trials took place near Liverpool in 1829. The prize for the winning design was £500. A crowd of 15,000 turned up on the day. They watched the five entrants run twenty times up and down the track – the distance of the return trip from Liverpool to Manchester.

TASKS...

Working in pairs, imagine you are one of the judges at the Rainhill Trials. Look at each of the three main competitors on page 37. Then decide which engine you think should be awarded the £500 prize, and why.

Note: to be eligible for the prize, the engines must:

- weigh no more than six tons
- be able to pull carriages equal to three times the weight of the engine itself
- travel at speeds in excess of sixteen kilometres per hour.

Share your decision with the class. Then take a class vote to decide the winning engine. Once you find out the real result, compare this with the class vote winner. Did you agree with the judges at the time? **WS**

The three main competitors

Engine 1: The Sans Pareil by Mr Hackworth of Darlington

Weight: 4 tons

Pulling power: 12 tons

Speed: unknown

Reliability: The boiler burst during the trial, so the engine was not able to complete its run; a compact design made the engine steady when travelling.

Engine 2: The Rocket by Mr Robert Stephenson of Newcastle

Weight: 4 tons

Pulling power: 17 tons

Speed: 22 kilometres an hour

Reliability: No breakdowns during the trial, so it was able to complete its run; a high chimney made the engine a little unsteady when travelling, which meant it swayed from side to side.

Engine 3: The Novelty by Mr Braithwaite and Mr Ericsson of London

Weight: 2 tons

Pulling power: 6 tons

Speed: up to 45 kilometres an hour

Reliability: Failed to complete the trials because the joints of the boiler gave way; however, the engine was light, compact and speedy.

After studying all the evidence, the three judges at the Rainhill Trials awarded the £500 first prize to the owners of the *Rocket*. The inventor of the *Rocket*, Robert Stephenson, won the contract to produce locomotives for the Liverpool and Manchester Railway and the railway line was opened in 1830.

How did the railways change industry and leisure time?

Railways soon became big business. Thousands of miles of track were laid by gangs of workers known as 'navvies' (navigators). By 1847 over 250,000 people were employed in the industry.

The coming of the railways increased the demand for iron and coal. Railway stations were built in towns and cities all over the country. London businessmen began to move to cities such as Birmingham, Glasgow and Manchester because they could now be reached quickly by rail.

The following statements explain how the railways changed people's work and leisure time.

1 Railways provided employment for thousands of men, particularly in the 1840s.

2 Workers began to live on the outskirts of towns (suburbs). They could go to work by train.

3 Many canals were no longer used and went out of business.

4 People could go on day trips and holidays by train. Seaside resorts such as Blackpool and Brighton became popular.

5 Railways transported coal cheaply. Coal became cheaper so it was in demand. The mining industry grew.

6 Railways needed lots of iron and steel, so these industries grew.

7 New railway towns developed, for example Crewe and Swindon.

8 A national postage system (the Penny Post) was set up using the railways.

9 Farmers made more money by sending fresh food to towns and cities by rail.

10 Football and music halls became more popular. People could travel to matches and concerts cheaply by train.

11 Cheaper coal helped the iron and steel industries to grow. They used coal for fuel.

12 People in towns had a healthier diet, as fresh food came from the countryside.

13 More people could read national newspapers delivered around the country daily.

14 Thousands of navvies suffered injuries or even died while building the railways.

15 Many homes were demolished in towns and cities to build large railway stations.

16 Until a new law in 1846 the width of railway tracks varied, making travel between different areas difficult.

TASKS...

1 The statements on pages 38–9 explain different effects of the railways on Britain.

   a) In pairs, sort these statements into two groups. The first group should show economic effects of the railways (things to do with money and industry). The second group should show the social effects (things to do with the way people lived their lives).

   2 Design a mind map using the outline suggested below to show the results of your thinking.

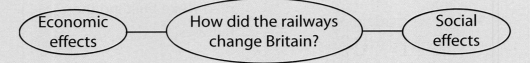

3 Look again at your mind map. Can you see any links between the different effects? If you can, link them with arrows. Write a simple explanation of why they are linked along your arrow.

4 On your mind map, highlight the effects you think are the most important. Then, write an answer to the question, *How did the railways change Britain?* In your last paragraph, write about which effect(s) you think were the most important and why.

Plenary

Talk about the effects that you thought were most important with others in the class. Make sure you explain your ideas.

Reach a class decision about whether or not the coming of the railways was a good thing despite the disadvantages.

WORKING-CLASS REACTIONS: DID EVERYONE AGREE WITH THE CHANGES IN AGRICULTURE AND INDUSTRY?

3

WHO WERE NED LUDD AND CAPTAIN SWING?

Objectives

In this section you will find out:
- who the Luddites and Swing Rioters were and what tactics they used
- why their protests took place
- how successful their protests were.

To find the answers you will:
- examine a range of sources
- think of your own ideas and exchange ideas with others.

Starter

Look at the two letters shown in Sources A and B.

SOURCE (A)

Sir,

We have been informed you own those hateful shearing frames. My men have asked me to warn you to destroy them.

If they have not gone by the end of next week, I will send one of my officers and 300 men to destroy them. We will burn your factory to ashes as well. If you attack my men, they have orders to murder you and burn your home.

We know your neighbours also have these machines. Tell them the same thing will happen to them if they are not removed quickly.

A letter to Frederick Smith, a mill owner, from Ned Ludd in 1812. A shearing frame was a machine that made the surface of woollen cloth smooth. This job had previously been done by hand.

This is to inform you that if you don't destroy your machines and raise the wages of married men to two and six pence a day and single men to two shillings, we will burn down your barns and you in them. This is the last warning.

A letter from Captain Swing written in the nineteenth century.

💡 *What are these letters complaining about?*

💡 *What are the writers threatening to do?*

Sometimes people turned to violence to stop changes taking place. In this section, you will learn about two examples of this type of protest.

Who were the Luddites and the Swing Rioters?

SOURCE C

A cartoon from around 1810 of Ned Ludd dressed as a woman.

The Luddites

Luddites were mainly industrial workers from Nottinghamshire, Leicestershire, Derbyshire, Yorkshire, Lancashire and Cheshire. Between 1811 and 1816, these workers destroyed machinery that was putting them out of work and making them poor.

Ned Ludd was the leader of the Luddites. One story says that he was an apprentice who destroyed his employers' equipment as revenge for a beating. He was said to live secretly in Sherwood Forest. He was almost certainly not a real person.

💡 Why do you think the cartoonist in Source C has drawn Ned Ludd like this?

The Swing Rioters

Swing Rioters were agricultural workers, mainly from the south of England. They rioted in the autumn of 1830 for higher wages. The first riots broke out in Kent and spread to twenty-two other southern counties.

The leader of the Swing Rioters was known as Captain Swing. It is unlikely that he was a real person. The name 'Swing' probably comes from the **flail** used in threshing, because it swings when it is being used.

💡 In what ways were the Luddites and Swing Rioters similar? How were they different?

SOURCE D

Why did the Luddites protest?

A modern photograph of a steam-powered loom. Women could operate this weaving machine. It put skilled handloom weavers out of work.

What effect did the new machinery have?

The Luddites protested about the introduction of new machinery in the textile industry. They were skilled craftsmen who had earned high wages and enjoyed a good lifestyle. Now they faced poverty because skilled workers were no longer needed – factory machinery had put them out of work. Many craftsmen thought that they could force the factory owners not to use the new machines.

Hard times

1812 was a hard year:

- bread prices had doubled since 1802 because of poor harvests
- people were not buying goods so wages fell
- the wages of hand-loom weavers had been cut by half
- unemployment was high.

Skilled craftsmen did not have the vote so they could not put pressure on the government to help them.

💡 Why do you think some industrial workers felt so desperate in 1812?

Why did the Swing Rioters protest?

At the beginning of the nineteenth century, farming was in a poor state.

- There were too many farm labourers and not enough work.
- Corn prices fell, which meant that farmers made less profit.
- Because farmers had less profit, they had less to pay the workers – this meant that wages fell.
- Between 1828 and 1830, harvests were poor. This meant that bread prices rose. So did the number of labourers out of work.

What effect did the new machinery have?

One of the main jobs done by farm workers in the winter months was threshing the corn. However, in the late 1820s and early 1830s, many farmers in the south of England started using steam-powered threshing machines. These machines did the work of many men. The use of machines therefore meant that farm labourers faced unemployment at the hardest time of the year. As a result, they hated the new threshing machines.

Farm labourers did not have the vote either, so they could not persuade the government to help them. They had to rely on poor relief (charity) to survive. To make matters worse, the amount paid in poor relief was going down and it was becoming harder to get help. This meant that the poor became even poorer.

💡 Why did farm labourers feel so desperate by 1830?

💡 Why do you think the Luddites and Swing Rioters thought that violence was the only way to solve their problems? Do you think they were right?

SOURCE E

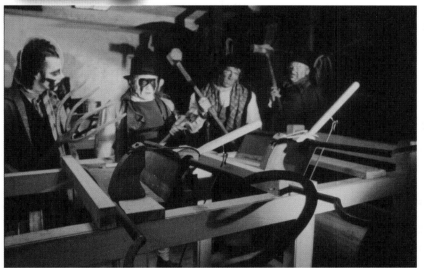
Luddites smashing machinery. The photograph shows actors from a television documentary, *The Luddites*, shown in 1988.

What tactics did the Luddites use?

Luddites attacked factories at night. They were disguised, often as women. They smashed machines, burnt down factories and sometimes attacked factory owners. Between 1811 and 1812, Luddites in Nottinghamshire destroyed about 1000 machines.

One of the most famous attacks by the Luddites took place at Brighouse in Yorkshire. The target was Rawfolds Mill, owned by William Cartwright. On 11 April 1812, about 150 Luddites led by George Mellor attacked the mill. However, unknown to them, it was defended by soldiers and two Luddites were killed. A week later, the Luddites tried to murder Cartwright. On 28 April, another Yorkshire mill owner, William Horsfall, was murdered.

💡 How do you think factory workers felt about their machines and workplaces being destroyed?

What tactics did the Swing Rioters use?

The Swing Rioters destroyed more than 350 threshing machines in the south of England. They also burned down many **hayricks** and damaged farm buildings. They sent threatening letters to farmers and even attacked some of them.

> ### Key words
>
> **Hayrick** A packed pile of hay.
> **Transported** Sent to live in another country such as Australia as a punishment.

How did the government react?

The government dealt severely with Luddites. Many politicians were afraid that they would cause a revolution in Britain.

The government sent nearly 12,000 troops into Luddite areas to help defend factories and keep order. Luddites were severely punished – those found guilty of breaking machines could be sentenced to death. Fourteen were hanged for the attack on Rawfolds Mill. Three were executed in York for the murder of William Horsfall. Fourteen others were **transported** as convicts.

Swing Rioters received the same treatment from the government. Some 2000 men from 34 counties were tried in court. Of those found guilty, 19 were hanged, 644 were imprisoned and 481 were transported.

💡 Do you think that the government over-reacted to the machine breakers? Explain your answer.

💡 Some historians say that working people protested only when they were hungry. Find the evidence to say that this was true in the case of the Luddites and the Swing Rioters. Do you think this violence would have happened anyway? Explain your opinion.

What did the Luddites and the Swing Rioters achieve?

The Luddites didn't really achieve anything. After 1820, they disappeared and the machines stayed.

The Swing Rioters did a little better. In some areas, wages did rise and some farmers got rid of their threshing machines. However, farm labourers' wages did not rise and they remained very poor.

TASKS...

1 You are going to produce a TV programme about the Luddites. Its purpose is to investigate the attitudes of people at the time to the Luddites.

   a) Divide into the following groups:
- a group of Luddites
- a group of factory owners who have bought the new machines
- a group of MPs
- a group of factory workers from a mill attacked by Luddites.

   b) Each group needs an interviewer and a script. Work on this together in your groups. Start with the questions the interviewer will ask and the answers that the group will give. Begin with a draft so that you can change things as people suggest new ideas.
       Try to include as much as possible of what you have learned as well as the ideas that you have talked about.

   c) Now put together your class programme. You can perform it as a play, or you could video or record it.

2 After you have performed your group's programme, look back together over your production. Do you all agree that it gave a true interpretation of the events and attitudes of the time? Think about your contribution. What did you achieve? How could it have been even better?

Plenary

Look carefully at the cartoon in Source F.

A cartoon of 1830 about the Swing Riots.

Does the source show that the supporters of Captain Swing used violence?

Who do you think is being threatened in the cartoon?

Look at the two characters on the right. What appears to be the difference in their attitudes towards the Swing Rioters?

Do you think the cartoonist was for or against the Swing Rioters? Explain your answer carefully.

WHAT WAS CHARTISM AND HOW IMPORTANT WERE THE CHARTISTS?

Objectives

In this section you will find out:
- who the Chartists were and why they protested
- how successful they were.

To investigate these ideas you will:
- create a diagram to show the causes of Chartism
- examine a range of sources to decide whether Chartism succeeded or failed.

Starter

Take a look at each of the six demands of the People's Charter.

SOURCE A

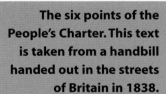

The six points of the People's Charter. This text is taken from a handbill handed out in the streets of Britain in 1838.

1. *A **VOTE** for every man over twenty-one years of age, who is neither mad nor a criminal.*

2. *SECRET **BALLOT** – to stop voters being bribed.*

3. *NO PROPERTY QUALIFICATION for Members of Parliament – men did not need to be rich and own property to become an MP.*

4. *PAYMENT OF MEMBERS of Parliament, so that working men could afford to be absent from work if they became MPs.*

5. *EQUAL **CONSTITUENCIES** – MPs should each represent an equal number of voters.*

6. *ANNUAL PARLIAMENTS – so that MPs could not bribe voters and buy their way into Parliament. No one would be rich enough to do this every year.*

💡 *What do you think the Chartists were trying to change?*

💡 *Which of these six points are law today?*

💡 *Can you think why one of the demands is not law today? Explain your answer.*

Who were the Chartists?

The Chartists were a group of working men who met together in 1836 and formed the London Working Men's Association (LWMA). Its leaders were William Lovett, Francis Place and Henry Hetherington. In 1838, they drew up the Charter and so became known as the Chartists. Chartism soon spread all over Britain. One group, led by Feargus O'Connor, set up a newspaper called *The Northern Star* to spread the Chartists' ideas.

What were the causes of Chartism?

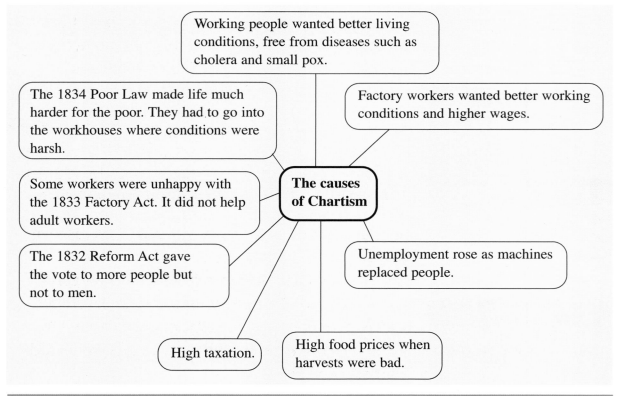

Working people wanted better living conditions, free from diseases such as cholera and small pox.

The 1834 Poor Law made life much harder for the poor. They had to go into the workhouses where conditions were harsh.

Factory workers wanted better working conditions and higher wages.

Some workers were unhappy with the 1833 Factory Act. It did not help adult workers.

The causes of Chartism

The 1832 Reform Act gave the vote to more people but not to men.

Unemployment rose as machines replaced people.

High taxation.

High food prices when harvests were bad.

Chartists believed that if working people could have the vote, they could do something about these complaints.

TASKS...

1 Look at the causes of Chartism shown on the spider diagram on page 50. Using a diagram like the one below, sort these causes into political, economic and social complaints. Use the overlap areas for causes that fit into more than one category. **WS**

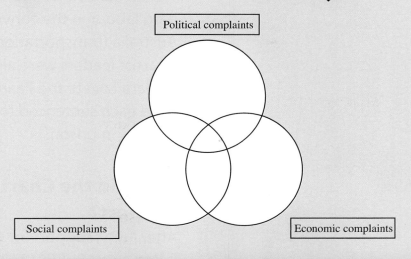

Political complaints

Social complaints

Economic complaints

What tactics did the Chartists use?

The Chartist leaders agreed about the demands in the Charter. They disagreed about how to get Parliament to accept them. William Lovett and his followers said that they should use peaceful persuasion. Feargus O'Connor and his followers thought that only violent action would succeed.

At first they used Lovett's plan. The Chartists presented a **petition** to Parliament. More than 1.25 million people signed it. However, MPs voted against the Chartists demands by 235 votes to 46. So some Chartist supporters became violent.

The most serious outbreak of violence took place at Newport, South Wales. A popular Chartist leader, Henry Vincent, had been arrested. On 4 November, local Chartists marched on the hotel where they believed he was being held. A force of special constables and soldiers stopped them. In the confusion that followed, shots were fired and many Chartists were killed.

Key words

Petition A request, often signed by many people.

The Chartist riot at Newport in 1839.

After the Newport Rising, ninety Chartists were arrested and eight were sentenced to death. However, this sentence was later reduced to hard labour in the convict colonies of Australia (transportation). Other Chartist leaders were also arrested. William Lovett and Feargus O'Connor were each sentenced to eighteen months in prison.

Why did the Chartists lose support?

After 1839, support for Chartism faded away. But in 1842, food prices and unemployment rose again. So Feargus O'Connor organised a second petition. This time, more than three million people signed it. Thousands of people marched to Parliament to hand over this petition. Once again, the government rejected it, this time by 287 votes to 49.

Some of these strikers brought their factories to a stand still. They removed the boiler plugs from the steam engines. So these strikes became known as the 'Plug Plot'.

The strikes ended quickly but 1500 strikers were arrested. Of these, 70 men were sentenced to between seven and twenty-one years' transportation. After 1842, Chartist support again declined as prices and unemployment fell once more.

What revived Chartism again?

In 1847, there was high unemployment. Food prices rose. Cholera and smallpox epidemics struck again. So Feargus O'Connor organised a third petition. This time, six million were said to have signed it.

On 10 April 1848, a mass meeting was held on Kennington Common in London. Chartist leaders planned to march with the petition from the Common to Parliament. Meanwhile, the government put 80,000 special constables on stand-by in case of trouble.

An engraving from 1848 showing the Chartist rally at Kennington Common in 1848.

O'Connor expected half a million people to come to the meeting. Only 20,000 turned up so there were more special constables than protesters. Only O'Connor was allowed to take the petition to Parliament.

In fact, only 1.9 million signatures were real. Others included Queen Victoria, the Prince of Wales, Sir Robert Peel, the Duke of Wellington and made up names such as Longnose, Pugnose, Flatnose and Snooks. After this, Chartism was not able to attract any support and so came to an end.

TASKS...

1 Why do you think so many people signed the charters in 1839, 1842 and 1848?

2 Do you think the Newport Rising in 1839 and the Plug Plot in 1842 helped or harmed Chartism? Explain your answer carefully.

3 Why was 1848 a disaster for Chartism?

WORKING-CLASS REACTIONS.

Was Chartism a complete failure?

1 Parliament refused to support the Charter.

2 Factory Acts improved working conditions for many people.

3 The middle class opposed the movement.

4 Chartists were divided among themselves.

5 Five of the six points of the Charter eventually became law.
- In 1858, the property qualification for MPs was abolished.
- The vote was extended in 1867, 1884, 1918, 1928 and 1969.
- The secret ballot was introduced in 1872.
- In 1885 electoral districts were made roughly the same size.
- In 1911 MPs finally got a wage.

6 Chartist demands were too extreme.

7 The 1848 petition made the Chartists look foolish.

8 In the second half of the nineteenth century, living conditions improved and towns became healthier.

9 Chartism was popular only when times were hard.

💡 Chartism only did well when times were hard. What does this tell you?

TASKS...

1 Take a look at the statements 1 to 9 above. Sort them into two lists:

a) reasons why Chartism failed

b) changes that Chartism helped to achieve in the long run.

TASKS...

2 Look at the two statements below.

> *Chartism was bound to fail because it did not have good leaders.*

> *Chartism was a complete failure. Working men had not achieved the vote by 1848.*

Explain how a historian sympathetic towards Chartism would answer these criticisms. Use the statements you sorted to help you.

EXTENSION TASK...

Try to find from your local reference library:
- if people in your area were badly affected by the changes in industry or farming
- if there were any Chartist supporters in your area or if there is any evidence of violence or unrest.

SOURCE D

Plenary

Look back at the six points of the Charter on page 49.

Choose three of the six points. Write a comment that a Member of Parliament at the time might have made about each of the demands you have chosen.

A contemporary cartoon commenting on the debate in Parliament over the Charter.

WHICH PROTEST MOVEMENT ACHIEVED THE MOST?

TASKS...

1 You are now going to consider which protest movement you think achieved the most and why.

To help you, copy and complete the chart below. Then fill in the chart with the information it asks for. Try to use your own words where you can. **WS**

Protest movement	Aims	Tactics used	How the government reacted	What the movement achieved
The Luddites				
The Swing Rioters				
The Chartists				

2 Now use the information in your chart to write a short paragraph summing up each protest movement. Which movement do you think achieved the most? Explain why you think it was more sucessful than the others.

Plenary

In small groups, suggest five ways in which people protest today.

Divide these into violent and non-violent methods.

Which method is likely to be the most successful? Why?

WHAT POLITICAL HURDLES DID PEOPLE HAVE TO OVERCOME TO GAIN THE VOTE?

WHAT WAS WRONG WITH THE ELECTORAL SYSTEM IN THE 1800s?

Objectives

In this section you will find out:
- the problems with the electoral voting system in the 1800s.

To investigate this idea you will:
- study the reactions of people towards the electoral system in the 1800s
- complete a living graph and diary planner.

Starter

Look at Source A below. Then read the statements of the five characters on page 58 and answer the questions that follow.

A political cartoon published in 1832.

The Reformers' Attack on the Old Rotten Trees; or, the Foul Nests of the Cormorants in Danger.

I am 35 years old. I own land and houses. Although I am very well educated, I am unable to vote because I am a woman.

A rich lady.

I am a landowner from Cornwall. I am very rich and rent out my land to local farmers. I have represented the people of Cornwall as an MP for many years, because I can afford to bribe the voters.

A landowner from Cornwall.

I am a rich industrialist in Manchester. I own several factories. However, I am unable to vote because Manchester has grown so quickly in size it has no MPs to represent us.

A rich factory owner.

*I work very hard farming the land to support my young family. I am unable to vote. They say it's because I don't own my own house and because I live in a **borough**, not a **county**. Why should it matter where I live?*

A working-class man.

*I live in a tiny old village with just ten other houses. I can vote – the village can elect two MPs to Parliament. Our village is called a **rotten borough**. Some say it is unfair that so few of us can elect two MPs.*

A property owner from a small village.

Hurdles to voting in the 1800s

MPs did not get paid so only rich men could stand for election to Parliament.

The growing industrial towns were new so they had no MPs at all.

Those who rented land sometimes did not live in the area but still had a vote.

Women were not thought sensible enough to vote.

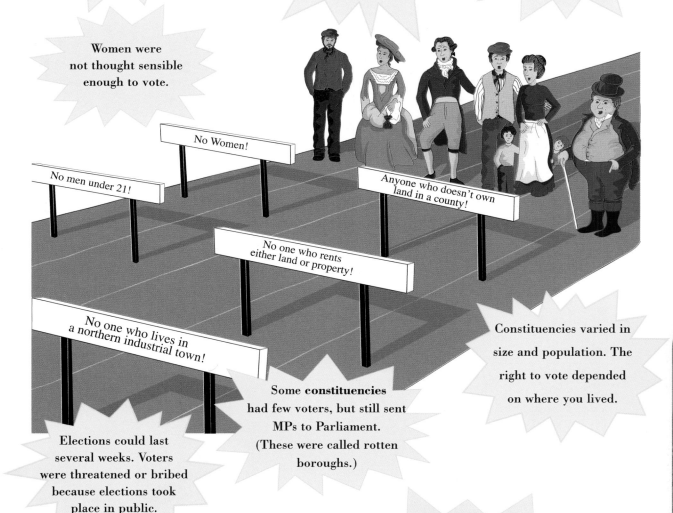

No Women!

No men under 21!

Anyone who doesn't own land in a county!

No one who rents either land or property!

No one who lives in a northern industrial town!

Constituencies varied in size and population. The right to vote depended on where you lived.

Some **constituencies** had few voters, but still sent MPs to Parliament. (These were called rotten boroughs.)

Elections could last several weeks. Voters were threatened or bribed because elections took place in public.

Some constituencies were controlled by one rich man. He would choose an MP by himself. These constituencies were called pocket boroughs.

Key words

Constituency The country was divided into areas known as constituencies. An elected MP represented each constituency in Parliament.

💡 *Which of the five characters do you think would find the system of voting unfair? Which characters would find it fair? Why?*

💡 *Do you think that Britain was a true **democracy** in 1800? Explain your answer.*

💡 *Look at Source A. On which side of the tree do you think each of the five characters would stand?*

TASKS...

1 Throughout this chapter, you will use a living graph and a diary planner to follow how the reform of Parliament affected the five characters you met on page 58.

a) Copy the living graph below into your book and plot the position of each character in 1800 onto the graph. **WS**

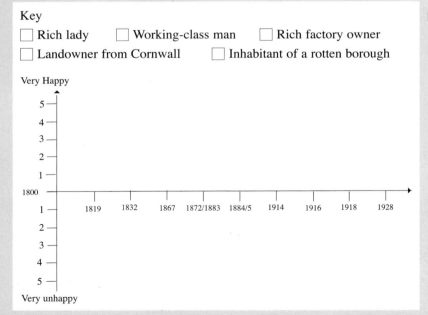

Key

☐ Rich lady   ☐ Working-class man   ☐ Rich factory owner
☐ Landowner from Cornwall   ☐ Inhabitant of a rotten borough

Very Happy

5 – 4 – 3 – 2 – 1 –

1800

1 – 2 – 3 – 4 – 5 –

1819 1832 1867 1872/1883 1884/5 1914 1916 1918 1928

Very unhappy

A living graph to show the impact of electoral reforms on individuals.

b) Fill in a diary entry for each character in order to explain:
- how the character would have felt about the electoral system in 1800
- why you chose that position on the living graph for the character. **WS**

Plenary

Write down five reasons why you think the electoral system in 1800 was unfair. Show your list to a partner. How are your reasons similar? How are they different?

WHY DID SOME PEOPLE BELIEVE THAT REFORM WAS NEEDED?

In this section you will find out:
- who believed electoral reform was needed
- why people believed that reform was needed.

To investigate these ideas you will:
- select and sort evidence and write a speech.

Starter

Take a look at the three characters below, then answer the question. You can find information about them on page 58.

💡 *Which of these characters do you think is the odd one out? Why?*

The electoral system in the early 1800s

In the early 1800s, more and more people wanted the vote. Life had become hard for many people after 1815 when the Napoleonic Wars ended.
- There were no jobs for the returning soldiers.
- Unemployment rose.
- Bread prices were high.

Many people wanted to voice their discontent. To do this, they needed to be represented in Parliament and to have a vote. However, not everyone wanted change.

POLITICAL HURDLES TO THE VOTE

Some opinions about the electoral system in the early 1800s

1 There is no need to change anything – our electoral system is the best in the world.

2 Only the wealthy landowners should vote: their land gives them status and everyone respects them.

3 MPs don't know about the needs of working-class people. The government only looks after the rich, and that's unfair.

4 The country will go to pieces if the masses are allowed to vote. They don't understand enough to have a say in how the country is governed.

5 Those who make the country wealthy, the businessmen and industrialists, should become MPs. They need to be involved in planning Britain's future.

6 The middle classes should vote. They will make our country more successful.

7 There must be new laws to protect the workers from poverty and unemployment and to improve their lives. This won't happen unless workers have someone to represent them in Parliament.

8 Why should only the rich become MPs? It isn't right that they can bribe their way into Parliament.

9 How can a borough with six houses have two representatives and a growing town with thousands have none?

10 A woman is not inferior to a man; women work hard to provide for their families.

Key words

The masses The large majority of the population who were working class and uneducated.

TASKS...

1   Look at the statements on page 62. Divide these into
    those for and those against electoral reform.

    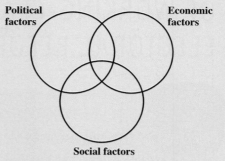

    a) Copy the Venn diagram (right) into your books
    twice. Above one of the diagrams, write the title:
    'Reasons for electoral reform'. Above the other, write
    the title: 'Reasons against electoral reform'.

    b) Sort the arguments for and against electoral reform
    by writing the statement numbers in the correct
    places on the two diagrams. Use the key words
    below to help you decide which category each statement belongs to.
    Some of the arguments may be two of these or even all three – you will need to write
    these numbers in the correct overlap on the Venn
    diagram.

2   **a)** In pairs, choose *two* of the three characters from page
    58 who have opposite ideas about reform. Write an
    argument between the two characters. One will need
    to argue the case for why things need to change. The
    other will say why they need to stay the same.

    b) Which of you won the argument? Did you change
    your mind or agree to differ?

    c) Perform your conversation to the class. Compare what
    you have included in your dialogue with what others
    have said.

Key words

Political factors To do with government.
Economic factors To do with making money.
Social factors To do with people's lives.

Plenary

In pairs or groups, discuss the following questions.

💡 Which character from page 58 do you think the government would take
most notice of? Why?

💡 Which character do you think the government would take least notice of?
Why?

HOW EFFECTIVE WERE THE CAMPAIGNS OF WORKING-CLASS MOVEMENTS FOR ELECTORAL REFORM?

Objectives

In this section you will find out:
- how working-class movements campaigned for electoral reform before and after 1832
- how successful these methods were.

To investigate these ideas you will:
- study evidence that shows the impact of electoral reform
- continue work on the living graph and diary planner that you began on page 57.

Starter

In pairs, look at Source A.

The Massacre of Peterloo by the political cartoonist, George Cruickshank, published in 1819.

Pretend you are one of the people in the picture, but do not tell your partner which one. Using the labels and the key words, describe what 'you' can see, hear and smell, and what your feelings are. Once your partner has found 'you', swap roles.

💡 *What three questions would you like to ask about what is happening in Source A?*

What actually happened at the Peterloo Massacre?

On 16 August 1819 about 60,000 men, women and children gathered at St Peter's Field in Manchester to hear Henry '**Orator**' Hunt and other reformers talk about the need to reform Parliament.

The local magistrates were nervous: the crowd was too large. The local **yeomanry** was present to keep order, as were the troops of regular **cavalry**. After Henry Hunt began to speak, the magistrates ordered the yeomanry to arrest him. The yeomanry moved towards the platform but the crowd tried to stop them. These poorly trained part-time soldiers drew their swords. At this point, the cavalry charged into the crowd to help them. The result was terrible: eleven people were killed and about 400 were injured, including women and children.

💡 How do the views in Sources B and C differ?

💡 Why do you think the views are so different?

SOURCE **B**

… prompt, decisive and efficient measures to keep the public peace.

The government's description of the local magistrates' actions in 1819.

SOURCE **C**

Over the field were strewn caps, bonnets, hats, shawls and shoes, trampled, torn and bloody. The yeomanry had dismounted – some were easing their horses … others were wiping their swords.

A description of St Peter's Field after the Peterloo Massacre by a politician who supported reform.

POLITICAL HURDLES TO THE VOTE.

TASKS...

 Imagine you are a newspaper journalist writing about the events at St Peter's Field. Your account has to support the view shown in either Source B or Source C. Use emotional language to support your viewpoint. The words below will help you with your report.

Examples of words that could be used to support the magistrates

brave
riot
attacked
provoked

Examples of words that could be used to support the reformers

cowardly
brutal
hacking
blood-thirsty
massacre

What were the effects of the Peterloo Massacre?

The government was shocked by the 'Peterloo Massacre', as it came to be known, and took action to stop large public meetings. The government also passed laws called the Six Acts in December 1819. Any hope of reform was gone – at least for the time being!

The Six Acts, 1819

- *Public meetings were limited.*
- *Newspapers and leaflets that might encourage public unrest were banned.*
- *Magistrates were given powers to search homes.*
- *Magistrates could try some cases in court instead of judges.*

TASKS...

1 Look back to page 60 to the living graph and diary planner that you have started. Remind yourselves of the five characters by re-reading page 58.
   a) Now use your living graph to plot the position of each character in 1819 after the Six Acts were introduced.
   b) For each character, explain in your diary planner where you have placed them on the graph and why.

How successful were campaigns for electoral reform after 1832?

Reformers could no longer campaign but some MPs, accepted that reform was needed. So between 1832 and 1884, the government passed a number of laws. These were meant to make sure that everyone was represented in Parliament. Most men were given the vote. But progress was slow.

The Great Reform Act of 1832
This made some changes.

- The new industrial towns were given 142 MPs.
- 356 rotten boroughs lost their MPs.
- 30 boroughs with a small population had one MP instead of two.
- One in five men could vote but they had to own property.

However, the Act of 1832 did not give voting rights to everybody:

- working-class men still could not vote
- having the vote still depended on where you lived
- bribery and corruption continued because voting was carried out in public.

The Second Reform Act of 1867
This made the following changes:

- some workers in towns could vote – but only those who were better paid
- industrial towns were given more seats
- small towns were allowed one MP only.

The Secret Ballot Act of 1872

By the terms of this Act:

- people could now vote in private
- voters could not be bribed or threatened
- those who tried to bribe voters were to be punished.

The Reform Act of 1884–5

This brought in the following changes:

- most men in most areas could now vote
- constituencies were roughly the same size, with one MP each.

These reforms meant that, by 1885, there were two million more voters in Britain. The electoral system was still not perfect but much had been achieved since 1832.

TASKS...

1 Look at your living graph and diary planner, which you last updated on page 66. Remind yourselves of the five characters by re-reading page 58.

   a) Now use your graph to show how the Reform Acts passed between 1832 and 1855 affected each character.

   b) For each character, explain in your diary planner where you have placed them on the graph and why.

   Which Act do you think was most important in making the electoral system fair?

   Explain your answer.

Plenary

Look back to the five characters outlined on page 58. Which of them would have been least satisfied with the Reform Acts? Why? Share your answers with a partner.

HOW EFFECTIVELY DID WOMEN'S SUFFRAGE GROUPS CAMPAIGN FOR ELECTORAL REFORM?

Objectives

In this section you will find out:

- the differences between Suffragists and Suffragettes
- the amount of opposition to women having the right to vote.

To investigate these ideas you will:

- use information to understand more about the Suffragists and Suffragettes
- use source evidence to discover who opposed votes for women.

Starter

Imagine it's the early-twentieth century. You want to join an organisation that campaigns for women to have the vote. However, you can't decide which group to join. Complete the questionnaire, which will help you to decide.

POLITICAL HURDLES TO THE VOTE.

Key words

House of Commons
One of the two Houses of Parliament where the members are elected by the people.

1 **You feel strongly about an issue and want people to listen to you. What do you do?**
   a) Try to persuade people to listen to your point of view. ☐
   b) Gain maximum publicity by making sure the newspapers write about everything you do. ☐

2 **You want those who live far away to know about your beliefs.** How will you do this?
   a) Distribute leaflets and posters, and hold public meetings with guest speakers. ☐
   b) Grab people's attention and make newspaper headlines by smashing windows and chaining yourself to fence rails. ☐

3 **You want MPs to listen to your cause. How will you achieve this?**
   a) Talk to them and send petitions so they know you are serious. ☐
   b) Harass them, enter the **House of Commons** and disrupt meetings so they are forced to act. ☐

4 **Someone fighting for your cause dies in an accident. How do you react?**
   a) You don't make a big deal of it. ☐
   b) You treat this person as a martyr, organising a huge public funeral procession to highlight your cause. ☐

5 **MPs have broken a promise to you and have changed their minds on a law they were going to pass. What do you do?**
   a) Carry on your peaceful protests because people are listening to your ideas. ☐
   b) Use even more violent methods – burn down a church and create more chaos. ☐

Key words

Suffragist A member of the National Union of Women's Suffrage Societies (NUWSS). They used peaceful methods to campaign.

Suffragette A member of the Women's Social and Political Union (WSPU), a more aggressive organisation that sometimes used violence to further its aims.

Suffrage The right to vote.

Spinster An unmarried woman. The term usually referred to women past the 'marrying age'.

*Now count up how many As and Bs you have scored. If you have chosen more As than Bs, you would probably join the **Suffragist** movement. If you have chosen more Bs than As, you would probably join the **Suffragette** movement. Read on to find out why …*

What was the difference between the Suffragists and Suffragettes?

Head of National Union of Women's Suffrage Societies (NUWSS): Millicent Fawcett, 1897

1867: middle-class and working-class women belonged to the organisation.

1897: there were more than 500 local branches.

1910: there were 21,571 members.

Petitions were presented to MPs in Parliament, leaflets and letters were distributed, and MPs were put under constant pressure.

The methods used were usually peaceful.

Organised speeches were held across the country.

Marches were well disciplined.

Many liberal MPs supported the suffragists.

We will get the vote.

Head of Women's Social and Political Union (WSPU): Emeline Pankhurst, 1903

1909: 11 regional offices.

Often associated with wealthy middle-class **spinsters**.

The methods used were often aggressive and violent.

Political meetings were disrupted; MPs were harassed and threatened with violence. Suffragettes threw stones at windows, burned down buildings, smashed paintings.

They took part in public debates.

We will get the vote.

Suffragettes were often arrested.

The Suffragette is the aggressive lady who tries to force Members of Parliament to listen to her. They prefer to spend time in one of His Majesty's prisons than in one of their own homes, although usually one stay in prison is enough.

The Suffragist is a much quieter lady. She does not believe in the aggressive tactics of the Suffragette, but is content to pursue her claims for a vote simply by her own persuasive speaking.

From the South London Press, March 1908.

SOURCE B

Suffragettes campaigning in London aganst the Liberal Party during the election of 1910.

SOURCE C

SOURCE D

Violent protests	5
Arson	11
Explosions	1
Window breaking	1
Telephone wire cutting	2
Use of chemicals	3
Meetings	89

An account of Suffragette activities in 1913, from the magazine The Suffragette.

A suffragette chained to railings near Downing Street in 1910.

POLITICAL HURDLES TO THE VOTE.

TASKS...

1 Look at the information on page 70 and Sources A to D.
   a) Make a list of the similarities and differences between the Suffragettes and the Suffragists.
   b) What do you think were the strengths of each group?
   c) What do you think were the weaknesses of each group?
   d) Which group would you support? Why?

2 Design a leaflet encouraging someone to join either the Suffragists or the Suffragettes. Write no more than twenty words on the leaflet.

What types of opposition did Suffragettes and Suffragists face?

In 1906, the Liberal Party came to power. Many women hoped that the Liberals would give them the **franchise**. However, this did not happen because most MPs still did not support giving the vote to women. In addition, many women did not want the vote for themselves: they were happy to leave political matters to men.

Key words

Franchise The right to vote.

In 1889 Mrs Humphrey Ward, a successful novelist, published an anti-suffragist petition that was presented to Parliament. She believed that women could exercise more power and influence in the home than any vote might give them.

From a modern history textbook.

Male doctors were prepared to argue that women are too emotional and prone to hysteria to be involved in politics.

An historian writing in 2001.

AN "UGLY RUSH!"

MR. BULL. "NOT IF I KNOW IT!"

[See Division on the Woman's Vote Bill.

A contemporary Punch cartoon, 'An Ugly Rush!' The man blocking the door to women's political rights is 'John Bull' – he represents the general British attitude.

What do you think is the message of Source G?

Who do you think the women standing quietly in the background are?

The violent actions of the Suffragettes succeeded in gaining much publicity for their cause. However, their actions probably did more harm than good. The public became aware of the arguments for votes for women. But people were shocked by the Suffragettes' violent behaviour. This meant that neither the government nor the general public supported their cause. The Suffragette's violent and aggressive methods turned many people against them.

Hunger strikes and forced feeding

Some Suffragettes were imprisoned for their violent activities. In 1909, one of these women decided to go on **hunger strike.** The government did not want the Suffragettes to have a martyr (someone who is willing to die for their cause). So it put a stop to this by releasing her. However, others carried on this protest.

SOURCE **H**

They could not all be released, so the government ordered them to be force fed. Women on hunger strike were fed through a tube, which was forced down the throat and into the stomach.

Forced feeding was dangerous. One woman died when the liquids went into her lungs by mistake. The Suffragettes used images of forced feeding to win sympathy (see Source H). This poster campaign was very successful. It not only told the public how badly the Suffragettes were being treated, it also showed how much they were prepared to suffer for their cause. So the government stopped its policy of forced feeding.

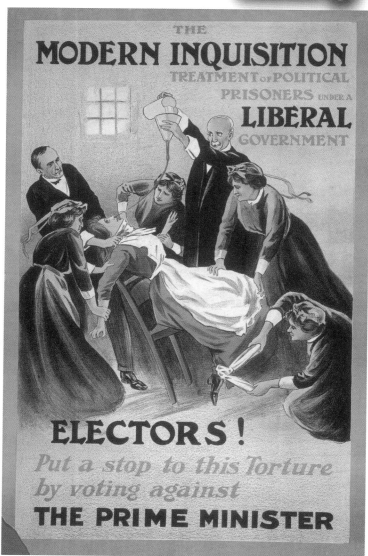

THE
MODERN INQUISITION
TREATMENT of POLITICAL
PRISONERS UNDER A
LIBERAL
GOVERNMENT

ELECTORS!
Put a stop to this Torture by voting against
THE PRIME MINISTER

The front cover of the Suffragette journal, Votes for Women, in 1910.

A Suffragette poster about the 'Cat and Mouse Act'.

The 'Cat and Mouse Act'

The government had to find a way to deal with Suffragettes on hunger strike and keep them in prison. So in 1913, a law was passed which said that women who went on hunger strike would be released once they became weak. However, they had to go back to prison once they had recovered. This new Act quickly became known as the 'Cat and Mouse Act'. It was given this name because, even when these Suffragettes were free, the government was ready to pounce at any time and have them returned to prison.

TASKS...

1 Look at Source I.
   a) Who does the cat represent?
   b) How is the woman portrayed?
   c) What is this poster trying to make people think?

2 Look at Sources H and I.
   a) What are these two pictures telling us about the way Suffragettes were treated?
   b) Did they deserve to be treated in this way?
   c) If you were asked to write the truth about how Suffragettes were treated, would these two sources tell you everything you wanted to know? Explain your answer.

How did the women's suffrage movement finally succeed?

1928: Equal Franchise Act
All women over 21 were given the vote.

'Votes for Women'

1928

1918: Parliamentary Reform Bill
Women over 30 who were householders or wives of householders were given the vote.

1918

1916: Representation of the People Act
All men were allowed to vote in elections held during the war. David Lloyd George became prime minister. He supported votes for women.

1916

1914: First World War began
Suffragists and Suffragettes end their political campaigns. Women take on men's jobs while they are away fighting. This shows men that they are capable and responsible.

1914

TASKS...

Look at the hurdles above.

1 Which event do you think was most important in helping women to gain the vote?
2 Look at your living graph and diary planner, which you last updated on page 68. Remind yourselves of the five characters by re-reading page 58.

   a) Now use your living graph to plot the impact of electoral reforms in 1918 and 1928.

   b) For each character, explain in your diary planner where you have placed them on the graph and why.

Plenary

Look at your completed living graph and diary planner.

💡 Write down at least three reasons why it was so important for people on your graph to have the vote. Share your ideas with a group or with the class.

💡 What reasons might you give to explain why people today should use their vote?

💡 Why do you think almost half of voters today do not vote in elections?

REVOLUTIONS: WAS THE PERIOD FROM 1750 TO 1900 AN ERA OF PROGRESS?

Conclusion

In this chapter you have studied revolutions in agriculture and industry. You have seen how people reacted to these revolutions and how conditions changed as a result. Now it is time to decide whether the period 1750 to 1900 was an era of progress. To do this, think about the situation in 1750 and the situation by 1900. How much progress do you think there had been?

TASKS...

1 Give each 'revolution' a score on a sliding scale of 10 to minus 10. Here are some guidelines to help you with your scoring.
   • A score of 10 means a great deal of progress had been made (progress).
   • A score of 5 means some progress had been made (progress).
   • A score of 0 means no progress had been made.
   • A score of minus 5 means that life had got worse as a result of the changes (regress).
   • A score of minus 10 means had got *much* worse as a result of the changes (regress).

2 Copy and complete the chart below. Use the score you gave each 'revolution' to decide how much of each column you need to shade.

	Agriculture	Industry	Working conditions	Transport	The vote
10					
5					
0					
-5					
-10					

3 Make a list of examples to explain the scores you have given. Then use your chart and your list to answer the question: *'How far was the period 1750 to 1900 an age of progress?'* Explain your answer carefully.

THEME: RIGHTS AND FREEDOMS

INTRODUCTION

💡 How 'free' are you? In small groups think about:

- things you are free to do
- how you would react if your freedom was taken away

- things you are free from
- how you might try to get your freedom back.

Share you ideas with the rest of the class.

In the next three chapters you will find out about groups of people in history who have been denied their rights and freedoms. You will also read about how they reacted to this. The timeline below will give you some ideas about the kinds of rights and freedoms that were denied some people in the past.

💡 Look at the timeline below and Sources A to E. What does this information tell you about the rights and freedoms that were denied people between 1750–1990?

TIMELINE
Rights and freedoms, 1750–1990

1709 Slave traders set out on their first voyage from Liverpool to buy and sell slaves.

1857 The Indian Mutiny: a violent rebellion against British rule in India. The British showed no respect for Indian religions, languages and customs.

1890 The Jim Crow Laws: black Americans are forced to live totally separate lives from white Americans.

1938 *Kristallnacht* (the Night of the Broken Glass) – a night of violence against German Jews.

1939 All Jews in Poland have to wear a yellow star, which easily identifies them.

1942 The Final Solution is put in place by the Nazis; this results in the murder of approximately six million European Jews along with about five million gypsies, Jehovah's Witnesses, homosexuals and other minority groups.

SOURCE A

A contemporary painting of a nineteenth-century slave auction in southern USA.

SOURCE B

A photograph of the separation of black people from white people in the USA in the early twentieth century.

SOURCE C

A photograph of Indian troops in France fighting for Britain during the First World War.

SOURCE D

A photograph of a Jewish mother and her children in the Warsaw Ghetto, Poland, 1943.

SOURCE E

A photograph of Jews being taken to a concentration camp during the Second World War, 1942.

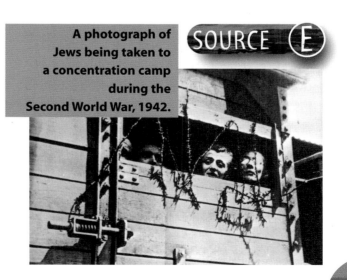

5 FROM SLAVERY TO CIVIL RIGHTS: WHAT WAS THE BLACK PERSON'S EXPERIENCE OF THE UNITED STATES OF AMERICA?

WHAT WAS THE SLAVE TRADE?

Objectives

In this section you will find out:
- how slaves were captured and transported to the Americas
- what conditions were like on the 'Middle Passage'.

To investigate these ideas you will:
- examine a variety of sources
- produce an account of a slave's experience of capture and the voyage.

Starter

Read Source A.

SOURCE A

Kunta thought he had gone mad. He awoke to find himself lying on his back between two men in the pitch darkness. He was naked and chained. It was unbearably hot. There was a sickening stink and a terrifying sound of shrieking, weeping, praying and vomiting. He could feel and smell his own vomit on his chest and belly. His felt pain all over from the beatings he had received since his capture.

A rat's thick, furry body brushed his cheek, sniffing at his mouth. Kunta struggled with the iron shackles that bound his wrists and ankles. He felt himself starting to vomit again. He lay wishing that he might die.

After a while, Kunta felt his shackled right wrist and ankle. They were bleeding. He seemed to be joined by the left ankle and wrist to some other man. The people were all so close to each other that their shoulders, arms and legs touched if they moved. There wasn't enough space even to sit up.

As Kunta lay listening, he realised that he wanted to empty his bowels. He had been holding on for days. He could hold on no longer.

Kunta was revolted that his own smell was added to the stench around him. He began sobbing. What sins was he being punished for?

From Alex Haley's book Roots (1976).

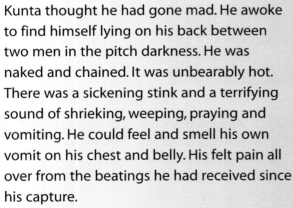

Alex Haley was an African American author. He traced his ancestors back to their African origins.

💡 *What other questions would you like to ask about Kunta?*

Write your ideas on the question wheel opposite.

Share your questions with the class. Explain why you chose them. As a class, decide on the six best questions. As you read on, try to find the answers to these questions.

What does it mean to be a slave?

Slaves were the property of their owners. The Ancient Egyptians, Greeks and Romans all kept slaves. Usually they were prisoners captured in war. After the fall of the Roman Empire, slavery almost disappeared except in Africa. Here, because of tribal warfare, some people became the slaves of more powerful tribes. These slaves were then sold to Arab slave dealers.

In some African tribes, slavery was a punishment for breaking the law. Sometimes, very poor people volunteered to become slaves because they knew they would be well fed and looked after. Slaves could also become free.

However, after 1440, European countries became involved in the trade in slaves. The Portuguese were the first slave traders. Britain and other countries soon followed. They realised that huge profits could be made from the sale of slaves from Africa. These Europeans created a new kind of slavery, one from which there was no escape. Children of slaves automatically became slaves when they were born.

Why did the Europeans need slaves?

By the late fifteenth century, European countries had **colonies** in **the Americas**. At first, local tribes farmed the land for the European settlers. However, the **natives** soon caught and died from European diseases. The settlers replaced them with a labour force brought by traders from Africa.

By the eighteenth century, the demand for slaves had grown so much that the 'triangular' trade developed. The map below explains how this trade worked.

Key words

Colonies Areas where people settle in another country.
The Americas North and South America and the islands close by.
Natives Local inhabitants of a country or area.

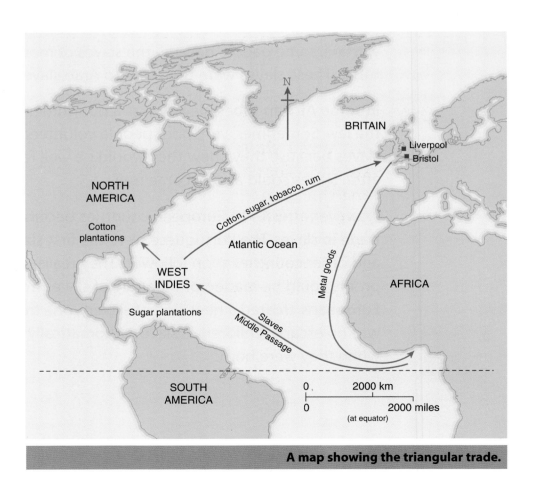

A map showing the triangular trade.

TASKS...

1 Do you agree with the statements below? Explain why or why not.

In history, slavery has always been evil.

Only black Africans were slaves.

What happened to slaves on the Middle Passage?

TASKS...

1 At the end of this section you are going to write a 'slave diary' about your experiences of capture and the voyage to the Americas. Begin by collecting the information you will need. Copy and complete the following planning sheet. Leave plenty of space so that you can add to it as you work through this section.

	People involved	Points for your diary
Capture		
The voyage		

How were slaves captured?

Slave traders got African slaves from other Africans. Tribal chiefs carried out raids to collect slaves from weaker tribes. These men, women and children were exchanged for goods such as alcohol, cloth, metals, jewellery and guns. Once slaves had been taken to the coast, they were kept in forts called 'barracoons' before being shipped across the Atlantic Ocean.

One day, the adults were out working. My sister and I were left to mind the house. Two men and a woman got over our wall. They seized us and ran off with us to the nearest wood. In the morning, we left the wood and took to a road. I saw some people in the distance. I called out for help, but my captors tied me up and stuffed me in a sack.

The next day my sister and I were separated. I was sold here and there, then moved on. After about seven months, we reached the coast. The first thing I saw was the sea and a slave ship, anchored, waiting for its cargo. I was taken on board and handled roughly by the crew to see if I was healthy. Their skin was a different colour from ours.

From Olaudah Equiano's autobiographical story written in 1789. Equiano had bought his freedom and settled in Britain. He became an anti-slavery campaigner.

The voyage to the Americas

The journey from Africa to the Americas became know as the Middle Passage. This journey took between six and twelve weeks. Each ship's captain had to keep as many slaves alive as possible. This was because his cargo was valuable – only those slaves which survived the journey could be sold. Sources C and D tell you what often happened during these voyages.

SOURCE C   SOURCE D

Below deck, the stench and crying made me so sick that I wanted to die. I was severely beaten. I would have jumped overboard, but we were being watched carefully. Two of my countrymen who were chained together somehow made it through the netting and jumped into the sea. Many more would have done the same if they had not been stopped by the ship's crew.

I had never before seen such brutal cruelty. One man was flogged so cruelly that he died; his body was tossed over the side as they would have done an animal. The heat and the overcrowding almost suffocated us. The air became unfit to breathe and brought on a sickness among the slaves. Many people died.

Written by Olaudah Equiano in 1789.

About 8 am, slaves were usually brought up on deck. If the weather was good, they stayed chained on deck until mid-afternoon. Their food was served in large tubs. About ten slaves would eat from the same tub using wooden spoons.

Those who wouldn't eat were punished. One captain poured molten lead on slaves, while another captain burnt slaves' lips by placing shovels of hot coals close to their mouths.

Written by a modern historian.

SOURCE E

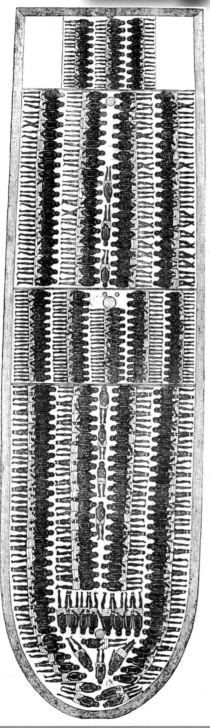

The Brookes was a slave ship originally built to carry a maximum of 450 people. In 1788, it was found to be carrying 609 slaves.

💡 Why do you think slaves were treated so badly if they were valuable cargo?

💡 Look at the drawing of the slave ship in Source E. It was used by **abolitionists**. What does it tell you about conditions on board this slave ship? From what you already know, is it giving you an accurate impression?

Key words

Abolitionists People who thought that slavery was wrong and should be stopped.

SOURCE F

The floor was covered with bodies packed together and between the floor and deck were often platforms that were also covered with bodies. The men were chained two and two together by their hands and feet. They were each allowed one pint of water a day. They were fed twice a day with yams and horse beans.

Written by Thomas Clarkson in a nineteenth-century history book.

SOURCE G

The filth of the lavatory-buckets made things worse. Children often fell into these. The shrieks of women and the groans of the dying added to the horror.

Slaves often went mad before dying of suffocation. In their struggle for air men strangled those next to them. Women attacked each other. So many dead slaves were thrown overboard that sharks followed slave ships from Africa to the Americas.

Written by Olaudah Equiano in 1789.

TASKS...

1 Add information from Sources C, D, F and G to the diary planning sheet you started on page 83.

2 It is 1788. You have been taken from your home by a raiding party and sold into slavery. You sailed on *The Brookes* slave ship (shown in Source E). Write a diary of your recent experiences, using the information in your diary planning sheet to help you. Write two entries in your diary.
- In the first entry, introduce yourself. Describe your capture.
- In the second entry, describe your experiences aboard *The Brookes* slave ship. It would be a good idea to have separate paragraphs on food, punishment, conditions below deck and what happened on deck.

Plenary

Look again at the accounts of the Middle Passage written by Alex Haley and Olaudah Equiano (Sources A, C and G). Make a list of the words and images the authors use to show you the horror of the voyage.

WHAT WAS LIFE LIKE FOR SLAVES ON A PLANTATION?

Objectives

In this section you will find out:

- how slaves were sold in the Americas
- how hard life was for slaves on **plantations**.

To investigate these ideas you will:

- examine a variety of sources
- write an account of a slave's experience of plantation life.

Starter

Read the following slave laws.

💡 *Why do you think plantation owners made these laws? Discuss your ideas with other members of your class.*

Key words

Plantations Large farms used for planting and growing crops such as sugar beet, tobacco and cotton.
Testimonies Evidence given in court.
Branded A mark of ownership or punishment that is burnt into the skin with a hot iron.

- Husbands may be sold separately from their wives.
- Children may be sold separately from their mothers.
- Slaves are not to be taught to read and write.
- Slaves cannot own property.
- Slave **testimonies** cannot be used in court against white people.
- Slaves are not allowed to travel.
- Slaves caught trying to run away will be **branded** with an iron.
- Slaves cannot gather together in groups.
- Slaves cannot carry weapons.

💡 *Plantation owners often preferred to buy a slave born into slavery than one newly arrived from Africa. Why do you think this was?*

How were slaves sold?

On arrival in America, the surviving slaves were sold to plantation owners. Their skins were oiled first and their wounds and sores hidden to make them look healthy.

Slaves were usually sold through auction. At the auction, slaves were sold to the person who offered the most money. Interested

buyers would be allowed to examine the slaves before making a bid (offer of money).

Families of slaves were often split up and sold separately at auction. Owners sometimes had their slaves branded before taking them to their farms or plantations to work.

A slave auction in nineteenth-century America.

Plantation life for slaves: the evidence

TASKS...

You are going to add information to your diary planning sheet that you started on page 83. At the end of this section, you will write the final entry in your diary. It will describe and explain your experiences of being sold at a slave auction and your life on a plantation. To help you write your final diary entry, continue using your planning sheet by adding the two new sections as shown below.

	Characters	Ideas for your diary
Capture		
The voyage		
Arrival		
Plantation life		

Most black people were slaves on plantations. In the southern states of America, many plantations grew cotton. Slaves were made to plant, tend and then harvest the cotton crops. Between 1793 and 1800, cotton production rose from 10,000 bales to 100,000 bales. Most of the cotton was bought for the cotton mills of Lancashire and Cheshire.

The slaves had to work long hours under the blazing hot sun. Often, children as young as six were forced to work in the fields. At night, slaves went back to their living quarters. These were often no more than run-down sheds where the living conditions were appalling (see Source C).

Some slaves were sold to owners who treated them well. Other owners were very cruel. They had complete power over their slaves. Even the 'best' slave owners sometimes used the whip to punish their slaves. Other forms of punishment were even more brutal (see Source D).

SOURCE B

The cotton picking season begins at the end of August. The workers must be in the cotton field at sunrise. You have ten minutes to swallow your dinner of cold bacon. You are not allowed a minute's rest until it is too dark to see. When the moon is full, you must work until the middle of the night.

Solomon Northop writing in his autobiography, Twelve Years A Slave (1847).

SOURCE C

Ten or twelve men, women and children were huddled in one room like cattle. There was no furniture. Our beds were collections of straw and old rags. The wind whistled, and the rain and snow blew in through the cracks. The earth floor soaked up the moisture until it was just like a pigsty.

A slave, Josiah Henson, describing his experiences on a plantation in 1849.

SOURCE D

Flogging of up to 75 lashes was common. Planters sometimes branded, stabbed, **tarred and feathered**, burned, shackled, tortured, crippled and **mutilated** their slaves. Thousands of slaves were flogged so badly that they were permanently scarred.

Written by a modern historian.

SOURCE E

Key words

Tarred and feathered This was when hot tar was put on the victim, who was then covered in feathers.
Mutilate To cut off parts of the body e.g. ears.

A contemporary drawing of a slave being punished by a beating.

SOURCE F

Africans are nothing but animals. They will love you better for whipping them, whether they deserve it or not.

A plantation owner in the nineteenth century describes how he treats his slaves.

SOURCE G

None of the evils of slavery is more horrible than the treatment of females. They are obliged to become prostitutes, to work as hard as men do and to become the breeders of slaves at the will and pleasure of their masters.

From the journal of Major J.B. Colthurst, published in 1847. Colthurst was a special judge sent to the Caribbean from Britain.

SOURCE H

Again and again the whip fell on his back. His cries grew fainter, until a feeble groan was all you heard. His head was then put against a post and his right ear was nailed to it. A sharp knife was used to cut off his ear and leave it sticking to the post.

Josiah Henson describes how his father was punished for protecting his mother against the sexual advances of the plantation overseer.

💡 What impression of plantation owners do you gain from Sources D to H?

TASKS...

1 Why do you think plantation owners treated their slaves so badly?

2 **a)** Add the information from this section to your diary planning sheet.
  b) Write the final entry in your slave diary about life on the plantations. Use separate paragraphs to describe your work, living conditions and punishments.

Plenary

Give five reasons to support what the author is saying in Source I.

What do you think a plantation owner might say in response to this criticism?

SOURCE I

The white people have robbed us for centuries. They have made Africa bleed rivers of blood! They have torn husbands from wives, parents from children, sisters from brothers and bound them in chains.

David Ruggles, a black bookseller from New York, speaking in 1834.

FIGHTING FOR THEIR FREEDOM: HOW DID SLAVES RESIST ENSLAVEMENT?

Objectives

In this section you will find out:
- how slavery was resisted
- how successful the resistance was.

To investigate these ideas you will:
- use sources to reach a reasoned conclusion
- produce a piece of writing that shows understanding.

Starter

Imagine a school assembly where the head teacher announces the following measures to take immediate effect.

- *There will be a 50 per cent increase in the amount of homework set.*
- *An extra lesson will be added on to the school day.*

Key words

Resist To refuse to accept something and oppose it.

*In small groups, try to think of five ways you could **resist** these measures without breaking any rules! Share your ideas with the rest of the class.*

💡 *What were the most popular methods of resistance? How likely would they be to succeed?*

Now repeat the exercise, but this time suggest how slaves might resist slavery. Share your ideas with the rest of the class.

💡 *Was this second list harder to come up with? Why?*

How was slavery resisted?

Slaves did try to resist slavery. This resistance took many forms. Some were more dramatic than others. Some had more success than others.

TASKS...

1 Copy the chart below into your book. You will fill in this chart as you work through this section, so be sure to leave yourself plenty of room.

Statement	Evidence to support the statement	Evidence to contradict the statement	Does the statement need changing? If so, how?
Passive resistance by slaves was successful.			
Slave rebellions rarely succeeded.			
Peaceful resistance to slavery was more successful than the use of violence.			

Passive resistance

Slaves often used passive (non-violent) methods to resist slavery. These included:

- working slowly
- producing poor quality work
- deliberately damaging tools and crops
- pretending to be ill to avoid work.

These methods reduced the owners' profits but could result in slaves being punished if caught.

Escape

Some slaves resisted by running away. If caught, they were brutally punished. Sometimes the letter 'R' was branded on the cheek or an ear or foot was cut off.

💡 Why do you think runaway slaves would be punished in this way?

💡 Which kind of resistance do you think most slaves tried? Why?

In the USA, some runaway slaves were helped by a secret organisation called the Underground Railroad. It was run by white people in the northern states. Escaping slaves hid in a series of safe houses, known as 'stations', during the day and travelled at night.

WANTED

HARRIET TUBMAN

$40,000 REWARD

Harriet Tubman.

Escaping slaves were guided by 'conductors'. Harriet Tubman became the most famous of these (see Source A). She had escaped from slavery herself. She made nineteen trips to the south during her lifetime and led 300 slaves to freedom in Canada.

Slave owners offered a reward of US$40,000 for Harriet Tubman, dead or alive, but she was never caught. Harriet was one of about 3000 black and white people who risked their lives to help slaves to freedom.

Because of the Underground Railroad, approximately 50,000 slaves escaped to freedom. However, as the Underground Railroad was secret there are no records of the exact numbers.

Rebellion

There were few slave rebellions. Slave owners were afraid of revolts and so punished rebels brutally. Slave rebellions did not usually succeed. However, the Amistad revolt did.

The Amistad revolt

In 1807, Britain and the USA banned the trade in slaves. Spain did the same in 1820. Despite this ban, the trade in slaves continued illegally.

SOURCE Ⓑ

Cinque, painted in about 1840.

In April 1839, Joseph Cinque and 53 other Africans were sold in Cuba to two Spaniards for their plantation. They were loaded on to the illegal slave ship, the *Amistad*, in Havana. While still in port, Cinque led a rebellion. The ship's cook and captain were killed and the rest of the crew were set adrift in a small boat. The slaves tried to force the two Spaniards to sail them back to Africa. Instead, the ship sailed towards the North American coast. The *Amistad* was captured in November by the US navy, and Cinque and the other slaves were arrested for murder.

FROM SLAVERY TO CIVIL RIGHTS.

Seventeen of the slaves died in prison. At their trial in January 1840, the survivors argued that they were free men who were being held captive. The jury agreed with them, and the judge ordered their freedom. However, opponents of the decision appealed. The appeal was heard by the **Supreme Court**. Cinque and the others were cleverly defended by a former President of the USA, John Quincy Adams. The Supreme Court agreed with the original decision. In January 1842, Cinque and the other Africans arrived back in the West African country of Sierra Leone as free men.

Key words

Supreme Court The most important court in the USA.

TASKS...

1 It is the appeal of the *Amistad* slaves in 1841.

   a) Imagine you are one of the following people: Joseph Cinque; one of the Spanish plantation owners who bought the slaves; John Quincy Adams; a narrator.

   b) Write a short speech for your character.

   - Joseph Cinque needs to say why he and the others have a right to be free.
   - The Spanish plantation owner has to argue why he thinks he has a right to the slaves.
   - John Quincy Adams has to persuade the Supreme Court that the men should be freed.
   - The narrator needs to explain the background to the case.

   c) When you write your speech, try to use words to persuade others such as *in fact*, *therefore*, *obviously*, *undoubtedly*.

EXTENSION TASK...

2 Use your school library to find out about Toussaint L'Overture and Nat Turner. They led two slave rebellions. How sucessful were they?

Plenary

Write down the five most important or interesting pieces of information you have learned in this section. Share your choices with the rest of the class. What were the similarities and differences in the choices you made?

HOW SUCCESSFUL WAS THE CAMPAIGN TO GIVE SLAVES THEIR FREEDOM?

Objectives

In this section you will find out:
- who the led the campaign in the USA to abolish slavery
- what changed for black people in the USA after 1865.

To investigate these ideas you will:
- consider the main arguments supporting and opposing slavery
- write a persuasive speech from one point of view.

Starter

Look at Sources A and B.

God loves coloured children as well as white children. The Saviour died to save them both. So, white children need to know that they must go to heaven without their prejudice against colour, for there, Jesus loves both black and white. Get rid of your **prejudice** and learn to love coloured children that you may be all the children of your Father who is in heaven.

From a speech by Sojourner Truth, a former slave, made in 1863.

Key words

Prejudice A narrow-minded view. Racial prejudice is when people are hostile or hate those of another race, belief or colour because they see them as inferior.

We only have to answer to God for slavery. Slavery has His blessing. Black Africans are intended to be slaves. They are totally inferior to us. They do not know how to use freedom. People only have to look to Africa to see how much slaves have gained by serving us.

The views of George McDuffie, the Governor of South Carolina from 1834–6.

- *Which of these sources do you think was spoken by a supporter of slavery, and which was spoken by an abolitionist?*

- *Read Sources A and B again. Which one has the strongest influence on you? You must be able to explain why. Share your ideas with others in the class.*

The American Civil War

The debate over whether or not slavery should be abolished went on for many years. People in the northern states did not agree with slavery (although they did not accept that white and black Americans were equal!). This meant that there was a split between the northern and southern states over slavery.

TASKS...

1 Find out more about the tactics the abolitionists used to campaign for the abolition of slavery in the USA.

People in the southern states were opposed to the abolition of slavery. Plantation owners claimed that slave labour was necessary to the success of their plantations. They argued that because they had paid for the slaves, the slaves were their property. Many white Americans believed that slaves were racially inferior and so had no need of human rights or dignity. Laws in America supported the rights of the plantation owners.

In April 1861, the USA was plunged into the Civil War between the northern states (the Union) and the eleven southern slave-owning states (the Confederacy). Towards the end of this war, in April 1865, President Abraham Lincoln announced his plan to end slavery.

The defeat of the Confederacy led to the following changes to the **American Constitution**:

- December 1865 – slavery was officially abolished
- 1866 – black Americans were given rights as **citizens** of the USA
- 1870 – black and white men were given equal rights to vote.

But did this mean that black people were really free?

Key words

American Constitution A document which states the legal rights of all Americans.
Citizen Inhabitant of a town or country with rights and responsibilities.

TASKS...

As you work through Themes 1 to 5 on pages 97–9, you will need to create information cards. You will use these on page 100 to complete a living graph. This graph will show whether the lives of black people improved after their **emancipation** in 1865

When you have completed each card, decide how much improvement there was for black people after 1865. Give each theme covered a score out of 10, as follows:

- a score of 10 means there was a definite improvement
- a score of 5 to 9 means there was some improvement, but there were still difficulties faced by black Americans
- a score of 1 to 4 means there was little real improvement, though some change
- a score of 0 means there was no improvement.

For each score, explain why you came to that decision.

> Theme:
>
> Score out of 10:
>
> Reason for decision:

Theme 1: Legal rights

By 1870, black Americans had been given the following rights by law.

- Equal **civil rights**.

- The right to vote and to stand for election.

- The right to sit on juries and become judges.

  - The right to legally own land.

  - The right to marry and have children without the fear of being separated from their families.

At first, the newly-won rights of black people in the south were protected by soldiers from the north. They stayed in the south until 1877. When they left, some **state governments** ignored the laws passed by the **federal government**. They persecuted freed slaves. Black people in the south soon lost the rights they had been given, including the right to vote.

Key words

Emancipation Freedom from slavery.
Civil rights The rights of each citizen to freedom, equality and the vote.
State government The government responsible for the affairs of one state.
Federal government The central government based in Washington, responsible for national issues.

Theme 2: the Freedman's Bureau

At the end of the civil war a Freedman's Bureau was set up to help freed slaves. It provided:

- more than 4000 free schools which taught about 250,000 black students
- health care facilities
- orphanages
- help for former slaves to find work.

As a result, by 1870, twenty-one per cent of black people in the south could read. However, after 1877 many schools for black people were forced to close. Some schools were burned and students were beaten up.

Theme 3: Sharecropping

After slavery ended, plantation owners had no one to work on their land. So they introduced sharecropping. They allocated land to former slaves who had to buy their own tools and supplies. The slaves received a 'share' of the crops they grew (only about one third). Black sharecroppers only benefited when harvests were good. Often, they got into debt because they had to spend more than their share was worth.

Sharecroppers at work on a plantation in the 1860s.

💡 Why do you think freed slaves became sharecroppers?

Theme 4: The Ku Klux Klan

In the years after the Civil War, terrorist groups such as the White League and the Ku Klux Klan (KKK) were formed. The KKK was a secret society set up by white people in the southern states. Its aim was to make sure that white people stayed in control.

The Klan terrorised former slaves or any white people who tried to help them. A burning cross in the night, long white gowns and pointed white masks were their symbols. Their victims were beaten, **lynched**, burned alive, shot or drowned. The Klan was banned in 1872. But judges and policemen in the south were often members, so the ban was difficult to enforce.

SOURCE D

💡 Why do you think the Ku Klux Klan had so much support in the southern states?

Theme 5: Segregation

After 1890, many southern state governments passed laws to segregate (completely separate) black and white people. This meant black people had to:

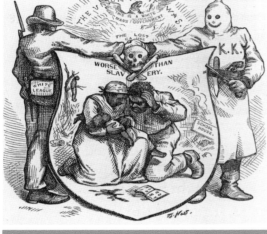

A cartoon from Harper's Weekly about the terrorist groups, the White League and the Ku Klux Klan, 1874.

- occupy separate seats in buses, theatres, and churches
- be treated in separate hospitals and use different public toilets
- send their children to different schools.

These were known as 'Jim Crow' laws.

Terror was used to enforce segregation. 2000 black people were lynched or burned alive between 1880 and 1900. Executions were advertised. Parents took their children along to watch.

SOURCE E

A photograph to show segregation in the southern states in the early twentieth century.

SOURCE F

The public lynching of Thomas Shipp and Abraham Smith in 1930. They had been accused of the murder of a white man.

SOURCE G

Southern trees bear a strange fruit,
Blood on the leaves and blood at the root,
Black bodies swingin' in the southern breeze,
Strange fruit from the poplar trees.

An extract from a song by the black jazz musician, Billie Holliday, 1939.

TASKS...

1 Plot the scores from the information cards you have been keeping on a larger copy of the graph. **WS**

2 Use your graph to help you decide if life had got better for black Americans by 1900.

3 'The abolition of slavery was successful. It brought about an improvement in the lives of black Americans by the beginning of the twentieth century.'

Write an essay to explain whether you agree with this view. **WS**

Use the information on your graph to help you write your answer.

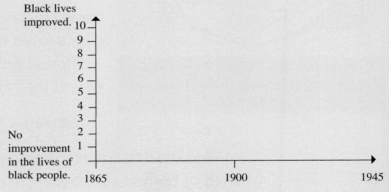

Plenary

Look at Source G. Popular songs are often used to give a particular message. What point is Billie Holliday trying to make in this song?

Is the song a fair summary of the way black Americans were treated in the period 1865–1900? Give reasons for your answer.

HOW SUCCESSFUL WAS THE CAMPAIGN FOR CIVIL RIGHTS IN THE TWENTIETH CENTURY?

Objectives

In this section you will find out:
- the problems that black Americans faced in the 1940s and 50s
- the success of the Civil Rights Movement
- the effect of Martin Luther King on the Civil Rights Movement.

To investigate these ideas you will:
- summarise success and failure using a range of evidence
- produce a documentary on the life of Martin Luther King.

SOURCE (A)

A photograph of a bus station waiting room showing segregation in the late 1950s.

Starter
Look at Sources A and B.

SOURCE (B)

A black man is kicked by a crowd of white men, 1943.

💡 What do these photographs tell you about the problems faced by black people in the 1940s and 1950s?

💡 Do you think photographs give you a true impression of these problems?

What was life like for black Americans in the first half of the twentieth century?

Prosperity and depression

Between 1900 and 1950, organisations were set up to fight for the rights of black people. Only white Americans enjoyed the prosperity of the 1920s. When poverty and hardship hit after 1929, all Americans were affected. However, black people suffered the most. By 1945, things had not improved for them.

SOURCE C

Black Americans queue for food handouts during the Depression, 1937.

The effects of the World Wars

When these wars ended, racial tension increased. This was caused by the competition for jobs and houses as black and white soldiers returned home. After 1945, black people became determined that they would end segregation, **discrimination**, poverty and violence.

Key words

Discrimination Acting against someone because of their race, religion or gender.

When did the Civil Rights Movement begin?

The Civil Rights Movement began in the 1950s . It campaigned to end discrimination and segregation, and for black people to have:

- the right to take part in government (including the right to vote in elections)
- an equal standard of health care
- an equal standard of education
- an equal protection by the law.

Read through the key events of the Civil Rights Movement below. For each one, think about:

- why it was a success
- why it was a failure.

Rosa Parkes being fingerprinted after breaking the bus segregation laws.

Key words

Boycott A form of passive resistance by refusal to make use of a service.

1955: The Montgomery bus boycott

On the evening of 1 December 1955, Rosa Parkes caught a bus in the town of Montgomery, Alabama. Segregation laws were very strict in Alabama. When Rosa refused to give up her seat to a white man, she was arrested and jailed.

As a result of Rosa's arrest, a meeting was held and it was decided to **boycott** the buses in protest. Thousands of leaflets were sent all over the city persuading black people to join the boycott.

Black people were the main bus users in Montgomery. This meant that on the first day of the boycott, nearly all the buses were empty. The boycott lasted eleven months. On 13 November 1956, the Supreme Court declared that segregation on buses was illegal.

SOURCE E

Elizabeth Eckford is jeered by a white crowd as she tries to enter the Central High School at Little Rock, September 1957.

1957: Resistance at Little Rock

In September 1957, nine talented black students joined the all-white Central High School in Little Rock. This was the school's first step towards the **integration** of black and white students. However, local white people protested. The Arkansas National Guard was sent to prevent the black students from entering the school.

In response, President Eisenhower sent 1000 paratroopers to Little Rock on 24 September. They escorted the black students to their lessons. However this did not stop the white students' abuse. Black students were insulted, their lockers were destroyed and one student had acid sprayed in her face. Nevertheless, in May 1958 Ernest Green became the first black graduate of Arkansas Central High School.

Key words

Integration The mixing of peoples of different races who had previously been segregated.

1960: The Greensboro sit-in

On 1 February 1960, four black students sat at an all-white lunch counter at a Woolworth store in Greensboro, North Carolina. They waited to be served. When the store closed that evening, they were still waiting. The next day, a larger group of students returned and the same thing happened.

Similar protests soon followed in other department stores across the south. If the black students were served, they moved on to the next lunch counter. If they were not, they continued to wait. If they were arrested, a new group of students took their place. White protesters attacked many of these 'sit-ins' and about 3600 protesters were arrested. Despite the attacks from white people, the black students maintained their peaceful protest.

White Americans pick on civil rights demonstrators holding a sit-in in a sandwich bar, 1960.

As part of the sit-in campaign, many black people in the north boycotted department stores. Consequently, many white people stayed away from these stores. They were afraid of violence. Storeowners lost trade so they eventually opened their lunch counters to black people.

1963: protest in Alabama

In April 1963 civil rights leaders organised a campaign of marches and sit-ins against segregation in Birmingham, Alabama. More than 30,000 people took part.

On 2 May 1963, a large group of black children marched towards the white area of town to protest against segregation. The next day, even more children marched. The police were ordered to use water cannons and to set police dogs on the marchers.

After three days, more than 2000 people, mostly children, had been arrested and imprisoned. Many Americans were shocked when they saw the actions of the police on their television sets. As a result, President Kennedy demanded that segregation should be ended in Birmingham. A week later, the council in Birmingham gave into the protesters' demands.

FROM SLAVERY TO CIVIL RIGHTS.

1964: the Civil Rights Act

This important Act gave civil rights to all US citizens.

- Segregation in public places was banned.

- Racial discrimination was banned in employment.

- An Equal Employment Opportunities Commission was established to investigate complaints of discrimination.

In 1965 the Voting Rights Act was passed. This ended racial discrimination over the right to vote.

How much had been achieved by the end of the 1960s?

Although black Americans now had equal rights:

- they continued to live in poorer housing and run-down areas

- schools and education for black children were inadequate

- unemployment among black people was high

- white people earned higher wages than black people

- black people still faced racist attacks from white people and were often the victims of police harassment and brutality.

TASKS...

1 Year 8 pupils are about to study the struggle of black people in the USA as part of their Citizenship lesson on rights and responsibilities. You have been asked to help them understand why it took a hundred years to achieve equality.

Work in small groups. Make three sets of cards.

- One set of cards is to show the opportunities black people had between 1865 and 1965 to make progress.
- One set is to describe the threats to success (the things that stopped them).
- One set is to describe events that brought about change.

You will need to decide how the pupils are going to use the cards to learn about the struggle for equality. For example, they could use them to create a large living graph on the classroom wall.

You do not have to have an equal number of cards in each set. You could make them attractive by using ICT.

When you have finished, compare the cards that each group has made. Decide which ones are the best. Put together a class set for Year 8.

What part did Martin Luther King play in the Civil Rights Movement?

Who was he?

Martin Luther King was born in Atlanta on 15 January 1929. He had a university education and then became pastor of a Baptist Church in Montgomery. He was also a leading member of the National Association for the Advancement of Coloured People (NAACP), an organisation dedicated to campaigning for the civil rights of black Americans.

The Montgomery bus boycott

On page 103 you read how an incident with Rosa Parkes started a bus boycott. King played a key role in organising the boycott. For this, he was arrested.

In response, King said:

The Southern Christian Leadership Conference

In 1957 Martin Luther King was elected President of the Southern Christian Leadership Conference (SCLC). In the next eleven years, King delivered more than 2000 speeches in different places across the USA.

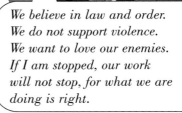

We believe in law and order. We do not support violence. We want to love our enemies. If I am stopped, our work will not stop, for what we are doing is right.

Leading the campaign for Civil Rights

Between 1957 and 1968, Martin Luther King made more than 2000 speeches in different places across the USA. He spoke wherever there was injustice, protest and action. He also wrote five books and several articles.

*Hate **begets** hate; violence begets violence; toughness begets greater toughness. We must meet the forces of hate with the power of love. Our aim must never be to defeat or humiliate the white man, but to win his friendship and understanding.*

> ### Key words
>
> **Beget** To produce an effect.

'I have a dream …' – the March on Washington DC

On 28 August 1963, around 250,000 people marched on Washington DC. Here protestors had gathered at the Lincoln Memorial. They heard King deliver his famous 'I have a dream…' speech. This described the hopes of the Civil Rights Movement.

Martin Luther King waves to marchers gathered at the Lincoln Memorial in Washington DC, 28 August 1963.

In his speech, King said:

> *I have a dream that my four little children will one day live in a nation where they will not be judged by the colour of their skin, but by the content of their character. From every mountainside, let freedom ring, and speed up that day when all of God's children, black men and white men, Jews and Gentiles, Protestants and Catholics, will be able to join hands and sing in the words of the old **Negro spiritual**, 'Free at last! Free at last! Thank God Almighty, we are free at last!'*

Key words

Negro spiritual A black American religious song.

The march on Washington was a great success. The success of the march and the tactics used by the Civil Rights Movement led to the Civil Rights Act of 1964 (see page 106).

Martin Luther King is awarded the Nobel Peace Prize

In 1964, Martin Luther King became the youngest man to be awarded the Nobel Peace Prize. He gave the prize money to the Civil Rights Movement.

The Voting Rights Campaign, 1965

In April 1965 King led 25,000 protestors from Selma to Montgomery, the capital of Alabama. Within a few months of the march, the Voting Rights Act became law in August 1965.

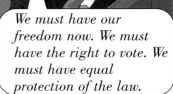

> *We must have our freedom now. We must have the right to vote. We must have equal protection of the law.*

Opposition to King

Martin Luther King did not win the support of all black Americans.

- Young civil rights **activists** did not always agree with King or accept his leadership.

- Some black leaders did not think that King's non-violent methods were effective. One of these people was Malcolm X.

- Malcolm X belonged to the 'Black Power' movement. It believed in the use of violence to achieve equality for black people.

💡 Do you agree with Malcolm X? How successful do you think his approach might have been? (Think about some recent examples of violent tactics e.g. terrorism.)

Don't try to be friends with somebody who's depriving you of your rights. They are not your friends. They are your enemies. Treat them like that. Fight and you'll get your freedom.

Assassination

In the spring of 1968 Martin Luther King travelled to Memphis, Tennessee. There he gave what was to be his final speech.

The next day, on 4 April, King was shot and killed by James Earl Ray while standing on the balcony of his motel room. Following his death, riots took place in more than 100 cities in the USA.

Martin Luther King's **legacy** lives on today in the USA. His birthday is a national holiday. The hotel where he was shot is now the National Civil Rights Museum.

💡 Do you think King's death strengthened or weakened the Civil Rights Movement? Explain your ideas.

Key words

Activists People who take action to get the changes they want.
Legacy What a person leaves behind after their death, for example gifts or the influence of their ideas.

TASKS...

1 Why was Martin Luther King a successful leader?

2 Why was King criticised by some black Americans?

3 Get into groups of six. You have been asked to make a TV documentary looking back at the life of Martin Luther King and explaining whether he made an important contribution to the Civil Rights Movement. Use the guidelines below to help you plan and write your documentary.

Decide what your documentary will show. Will it support the work of Martin Luther King, will it be critical of his work, or will it give a balanced view?

Your documentary should include:

- the key events in the life of Martin Luther King
- an interview with Martin Luther King explaining his ideas and beliefs
- interviews with leading figures such as Rosa Parks, who explain why Martin Luther King is so important
- an interview with Malcolm X who will question Martin Luther King's methods
- a conclusion in which you will decide on the importance of Martin Luther King in the history of the Civil Rights Movement in the USA.

Use a larger copy of this planning sheet to help you plan and write your documentary.

Scene: Explain who will be in the shot/what the shot will show:	Long shot
	Close up
	Other
Commentary/script:	

4 a) Present your ideas to the rest of the class. As you watch each other's presentations, make a note of how their views are different to yours. Have a class discussion about the differences.

b) Decide how well other groups have used the information and presented their ideas. Your teacher will help you to organise this.

Key words

Epitaph A brief statement summarising the life and work of somebody who has died.

Plenary

If you had to write an **epitaph** of no more than 20 words to go on the tombstone of Martin Luther King, what would it be? Share your ideas with the rest of the class.

HOW 'GREAT' WAS THE BRITISH EMPIRE?

6

DID EVERYONE BENEFIT FROM THE 'GREAT' BRITISH EMPIRE?

Objectives

In this section you will find out:
- why Britain wanted an empire in the nineteenth century
- whether everyone benefited from being part of the British Empire.

To investigate these ideas you will:
- select and organise evidence.

Starter

Look carefully at Source A and read Source B.

SOURCE **A**

SOURCE **B**

In June every year, British people celebrated 'Empire Day'. This photo is from an Empire Day celebration in 1922.

We are the British, engaged in the magnificent work of governing an inferior race.

Said by Lord Mayo, Viceroy (governor) of India from 1869–72.

Why do you think British people celebrated Empire Day each year?

Which of these words decscribes Lord Mayo's statement in Source B: ashamed, angry, sad, proud, superior? (You can choose more than one word.)
Explain your choice.

What was the British Empire?

In the nineteenth and early twentieth centuries, Britain had the biggest empire in the world. An empire is a group of countries (called colonies) ruled by one 'mother' country. Britain's empire covered about one-quarter of the world's land surface. The map below shows all the colonies in the British Empire at the beginning of the twentieth century.

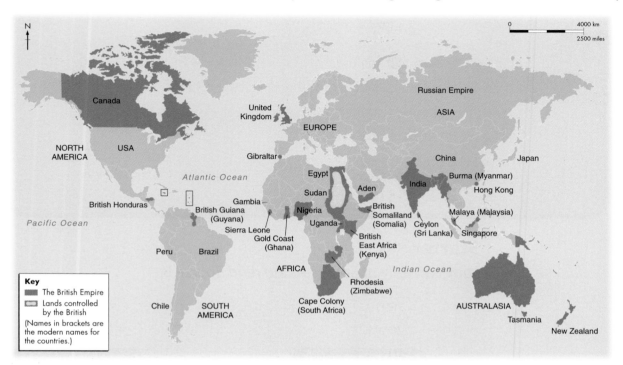

A map of the British Empire in 1900.

The benefits of the British Empire

Read the account of a young boy's typical day in the British Empire.

> The young boy woke up, got out of bed, pulled on his trousers and his <u>woolly</u> jumper. He had a cup of <u>tea</u> and a bowl of Shredded <u>Wheat</u> for breakfast. Then he put on his <u>rubber</u>-soled shoes and went to school. When he got home, his mum had made <u>lamb curry</u> for dinner – his favourite. At bedtime, the boy had a mug of hot <u>cocoa</u>.

This young boy's day is similar to that of many people living in Britain. You probably eat and wear some of the things that he does. Many of the items underlined originally came from British colonies.

Britain could get cheap **raw materials** from the colonies. This is one of the reasons why Britain benefited from having a large empire.

 List any other reasons why countries like Britain wanted an empire in the nineteenth century.

Why did the British Empire grow between 1750 and 1900?

There were several reasons why Britain's empire grew between 1750 and 1900.

Trade

British merchants had bought goods from many countries since the seventeenth century. Companies like the British East India Company organised this trade. The British government gradually became involved and then took over many of these countries, making them part of its empire.

Religion

Many people in Britain thought that the native people of some countries were 'uncivilised'. They could send **missionaries** to convert the native peoples of the empire to Christianity.

Exploration

Adventurers were attracted by the idea of finding new lands to add to Britain's empire. Stories of exploration interested people at home.

A map of the countries that controlled Africa by 1900.

Key
- British
- French
- German
- Portuguese
- Belgian
- Italian
- Spanish

MOROCCO, TUNISIA, Suez Canal, ALGERIA, LIBYA, RIO DE ORIO, EGYPT, SENEGAL, GAMBIA, FRENCH GUINEA, FRENCH EQUATORIAL AFRICA, ANGLO-EGYPTIAN SUDAN, ERITREA, DAHOMEY, PORTUGUESE GUINEA, BRITISH SOMALILAND, GOLD COAST, NIGERIA, ABYSSINIA, CAMEROONS, SIERRA LEONE LIBERIA, TOGO, ITALIAN SOMALILAND, SPANISH GUINEA, GABON, UGANDA, KENYA, CONGO, GERMAN EAST AFRICA, ANGOLA, NORTHERN RHODESIA, MOZAMBIQUE, GERMAN SOUTH WEST AFRICA, SOUTHERN RHODESIA, SOUTH AFRICA, Cape of Good Hope

0   500 km
310 miles

Competition for empire

European countries competed with each other to have the biggest empire. Competition for African colonies led to the 'Scramble for Africa'. By 1900, European countries controlled 90 per cent of Africa.

Resources

Colonies could also provide Britain with:

- cheap labour
- soldiers
- a market for goods.

Men sometimes died fighting for the country that controlled them. These headstones are from a New Zealand First World War graveyard.

TASKS...

1 Copy and complete the mind map below. Add details around each big reason to show why you think Britain would have benefited from having an empire.

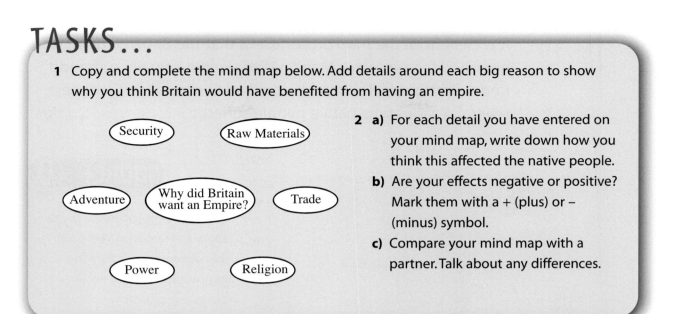

Security

Raw Materials

Adventure

Why did Britain want an Empire?

Trade

Power

Religion

2 a) For each detail you have entered on your mind map, write down how you think this affected the native people.

b) Are your effects negative or positive? Mark them with a + (plus) or − (minus) symbol.

c) Compare your mind map with a partner. Talk about any differences.

Did everyone benefit from the British Empire?

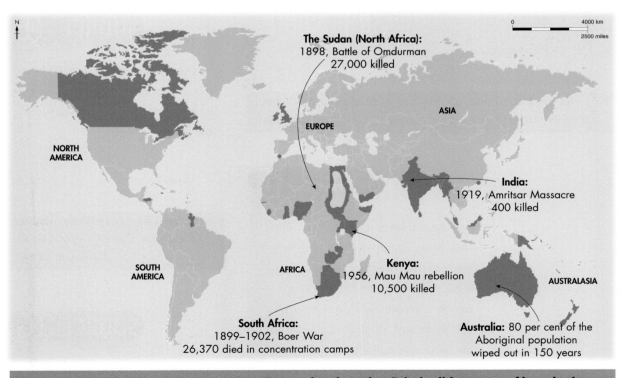

The Sudan (North Africa):
1898, Battle of Omdurman
27,000 killed

ASIA

EUROPE

NORTH AMERICA

India:
1919, Amritsar Massacre
400 killed

SOUTH AMERICA

AFRICA

Kenya:
1956, Mau Mau rebellion
10,500 killed

AUSTRALASIA

South Africa:
1899–1902, Boer War
26,370 died in concentration camps

Australia: 80 per cent of the Aboriginal population wiped out in 150 years

0   4000 km
2500 miles

A map showing what Britain did to some of its colonies.

💡 What does the map tell us about how native people thought of the British Empire?

It is clear from the map on page 115 that the British Empire was not good for everyone. Many native people actually suffered under British rule. The map below and Sources D to G suggest several reasons why native people suffered.

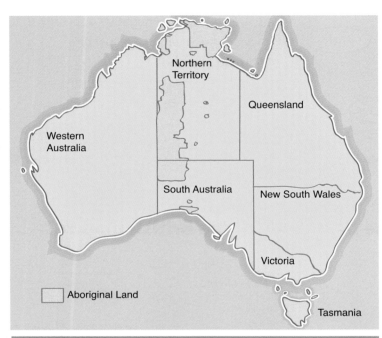

The land Australian Aborigines were allowed to live on. British settlers were known to hunt Aborigines for sport.

The native people became cheap labour and remained very poor. They did not benefit from the huge profits that their British rulers were making.

From a modern history book.

This is my view of the native. I have made up my mind. The native is to be treated as a child and denied the vote.

Said by Cecil Rhodes, Prime Minister of Cape Colony (South Africa), in 1894.

Can these thieves really be our rulers? They bring a huge number of goods, made in their own country, and sell them in our markets. They steal our wealth and take life from our people. Can those who steal the harvest from our fields and doom us to hunger, fever and plague really be our rulers? Can foreigners really be our rulers, who make us pay even more taxes?

Leaflet written in Bengal, 1907.

British customs were sometimes forced on the native people and local customs, culture and religions were ignored.

From a modern history book.

TASKS...

Look at the map on page 116 and Sources D to G. Each one suggests a different reason why some native people did not always benefit from British rule.

1 Copy and complete the mind map (right) to show these reasons. The question you need to answer is at the centre of the mind map. Find one reason from the map and each of the sources. Add it to the mind map. Try to explain each reason. If you think some of your reasons are linked, draw lines to join them on your mind map. Try to explain each link.

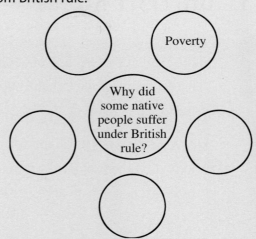

Poverty

Why did some native people suffer under British rule?

2 Compare your mind map with a partner's. Do you think you need to change yours in any way? Explain why.

Plenary

Look at Source H, then answer the questions that follow.

We British gave our colonies law and order. We took freedom, justice and democracy to the native peoples. We gave them the benefits of technology.

What were these advantages? First – easy travel; second – education; third – public health. In addition to the fight against disease, our experts helped to provide sanitation and pure water supplies. There were also improvements in agriculture.

A British government official, writing in the twentieth century.

● Is this source telling a different story to the other evidence in this section?

● Why do you think the author of Source H might not be telling the whole truth?

HOW SUCCESSFULLY DID LOCAL PEOPLE RESIST BRITISH RULE?

Objectives

In this section you will find out about:
- life for people living in India under British rule
- two conflicts between the British and the Indians.

To investigate these ideas you will:
- look at methods of protest and resistance against the British
- take part in a debate or discussion.

Starter

Look at Source A.

SOURCE A

The Indian leader Mohandas Gandhi leading the Salt March in 1930.

Try to think of three questions you would like to ask about this picture so that you can find out more.

TIMELINE
British rule in India, 1756–1947

1756   The Black Hole of Calcutta: the ruler of Bengal attacks a British settlement in Calcutta. 146 people are imprisoned in a space measuring 6 metres by 8 metres with no water. Overnight, 123 of them die.

1757   The Battle of Plassey: Robert Clive leads his troops to victory against the ruler of Bengal. The British East India Company now has almost complete control of India.

1833   The English language is taught to Indian children.

1857   The Indian Mutiny: there is a violent rebellion against the British in India. Indians attack the families of British troops and some 200 women and children are killed (see Source B).

SOURCE **B**

British officers and their wives are shown being attacked during the Indian Mutiny. From a book published in 1858.

1858   The British government takes control of India from the British East India Company. India is now part of the British Empire.

1861   Indians are allowed to hold positions on councils and to become magistrates (supervise legal decisions).

1877   Queen Victoria is given the title 'Empress of India'.

1885   The Indian National Congress is formed to represent the Indian people.

1914 The First World War begins. As citizens of the empire, Indian soldiers are sent to fight in the trenches in France and Belgium (see Source C).

1919 13 April, the Amritsar Massacre: British soldiers fire on a peaceful protest against British rule. 400 men, women and children are killed. This is met with national outrage. The Government of India Act is passed. It sets up a new government made up of Indian and British representatives. But the Act is unacceptable because only wealthy Indians can vote.

1920 Mohandas Gandhi becomes leader of the Indian National Congress. He plans a huge, peaceful campaign against British rule in India.

1930 Gandhi leads another peaceful protest called the Salt March (see Source A).

1935 The Second Government of India Act sets up Parliaments in eleven provinces. All Indians are given the vote, but Britain still remains in control. The Indian National Congress opposes the Act.

1939 The Second World War begins. Britain declares that India is at war with Germany. The Indian National Congress does not want this.

1947 15 August: India becomes independent.

A photograph of Indian troops in France during the First World War.

Independence Day celebrations in India, 15 August 1947.

In the pages that follow (pages 121–4), you will look at two events from the timeline on pages 119–20 to compare their successes and failures.

The Indian Mutiny, 1857

British influence in India began with the British East India Company. The company set up its own army to protect its interests. This was made up of Indian soldiers commanded by British officers.

Many Indians disliked British control and the attempts by British missionaries to spread Christianity. In 1857, the British introduced a new type of rifle into the Indian army. The Indian soldiers were told to grease the rifle with cow and pig fat. This was extremely offensive to **Hindus** and **Muslims**.

Once the mistake had been recognised, Indian soldiers were told to use vegetable oil instead. However, the damage had already been done. In May 1857, an Indian soldier shot his British officer and the violence quickly spread.

This mutiny was a serious threat to British power in India.

TASKS...

1 What do you think the British government should have done about the Indian Mutiny?

Write down some possible solutions and decide on the best one.
Share your ideas with the person next to you.

How successful was the Indian Mutiny?

The Indian Mutiny did not force the British out of India. Does this mean that it was a complete failure?

> *What a waste of time! Indians died in the violence. There was even more British control afterwards, not less. It shattered any hope of India becoming independent.*

> *We showed the British that if they want to stay in India, they must show some respect for us and our beliefs.*

TASKS...

1 The statements in the speech bubbles show two opposite views about the results of the Indian Mutiny. Which side do you think is closest to the truth? Why?

2 Look at the following statements. Read each one and decide which viewpoint each statement supports. **WS**

a) The mutiny did not spread throughout the country.

b) Sikh soldiers remained loyal to the British.

c) The mutiny made the British more determined to defend their empire.

d) The leader of the rebellion was a poor leader and general.

e) The British massacred innocent people, including women and children.

f) British authority collapsed in some areas.

g) The mutiny created bitterness between Indians and the British.

h) Some things changed: the British showed more respect for the different religions in India; Indians were allowed to hold government jobs.

i) The Indian rebels were very violent towards the British.

j) In 1858, Britain abolished the East India Company and took full control of India.

Key words

Sikhs Followers of Sikhism.

The Salt March, 1930

By 1930, many Indians wanted to drive the British out of India and rule for themselves. The campaign for Indian independence was led was Mohandas Gandhi. He was sometimes known by his people as 'Mahatma', which means 'Great Soul'.

Gandhi was a devout Hindu. Hindus are against violence and killing, so Gandhi tried to achieve independence by using **passive resistance**. The most famous example of this was the Salt March of 1930 (see Source A on page 118).

(see Source A on page 118)

Key words

Passive resistance To oppose or refuse to obey laws without using violence.

Indians were made to buy salt at high prices from British companies. It would have been cheaper if they had been allowed to make salt themselves. In March 1930, Gandhi began a 200-mile march to the sea. He was joined by thousands of followers along the way. When he got there he simply bent down and picked up a chunk of sea salt from the shore.

💡 What point do you think Gandhi was trying to make when he picked up the sea salt?

💡 What does this tell you about Gandhi?

TASKS...

1 How would you advise the British government to react to Gandhi's actions? Note down some possible solutions.

How successful was the Salt March?

The Salt March was a great success. It proved that ordinary Indians could bring about change in a non-violent way.

Peaceful Indians died or were sent to jail as a result of this 'non-violence'. It failed to drive the British out of India.

TASKS...

1 Which of the statements on page 123 do you think is closest to the truth?

2 Look at the following statements. Read each one and decide which viewpoint each statement supports.

a) The protesters proved that passive resistance could result in change.

b) Many ordinary Indians followed Gandhi's example. About 100,000 people were arrested.

c) The British reacted violently; police beat up unarmed protesters. This reduced resistance in some areas.

d) Changes were made to the salt laws. The British could not keep putting people in prison.

e) The British were not driven out of India.

f) Large communities of Indians did not join in the protest.

g) The army's violent reaction to a peaceful protest showed Britain in a bad light. The protest showed that many Indians were not happy with British rule in India.

h) Gandhi's non-violent protest sparked off violent riots in some parts of India.

i) Britain agreed to negotiate with Gandhi and the Indian National Congress for the first time.

j) The Salt March brought worldwide publicity to India's campaign for independence.

Once you have sorted the statements, you should reach a final judgement on how successful the Salt March was. Weigh up the evidence on each side and write a conclusion, saying which viewpoint you support and why.

Plenary

SOURCE E

England can rule India only if the Indian people agree to it. We can't rule it by the sword.

Sir Charles Innes, a provincial governor of India.

Do you agree with this statement? Discuss it as a class.

HOW DID LIFE CHANGE FOR JEWS LIVING IN EUROPE, 1919–45?

7

The Holocaust: facts and figures

Victims of persecution

78,000 The number of Jews who left Germany in the first three years of Nazi rule.

18,000 The number of Jewish children sent to safety in Britain.

170,000 The number of people murdered in the Nazi **euthanasia** programme.

Victims of Auschwitz

3 months The average life expectancy in Auschwitz, the largest Nazi concentration camp.

2000 The number of people cremated at Auschwitz every day.

3 to 15 minutes The time it took to kill 1000 people in a gas chamber at Auschwitz.

38,000 The number of pairs of men's shoes found at Auschwitz.

836,255 The number of women's dresses found at Auschwitz.

Victims of the Holocaust

6 million The number of Jews who died.

5.5 million Other people killed by the Nazis including gypsies, homosexuals, **Jehovah's Witnesses**, the physically and mentally handicapped.

1.5 million The number of children who perished.

> ### Key words
> **Euthanasia** Ending someone's life prematurely.
> **Jehovah's Witnesses** A religious group.

Look carefully at the figures and statements above.

💡 *Write down the questions these statements and figures make you want to ask about the Holocaust.*

💡 *Share your questions with the rest of the class. Use these questions to make a plan for your research into the Holocaust. Read on to find the answers.*

HOW DID THE EXPERIENCES OF JEWS LIVING IN GERMANY CHANGE BETWEEN 1919 AND 1945?

Objectives

In this section you will find out:
- how Jewish people's experiences changed in Germany between 1919 and 1945
- the methods used by Adolf Hitler to encourage people to hate Jews.

To investigate these ideas you will:
- make a comparison of sources
- create a mind map to show the changes over a period of time.

Starter
Read Sources A and B, then answer the questions that follow.

SOURCE A

Jews and Germans killed during the First World War were buried side by side. This graveyard is in Germany.

SOURCE B

A poster published in 1920 which explains that over 12,000 German Jews were killed fighting for their country in the First World War.

💡 What do you think that Sources A and B are suggesting to you about the Jews in Germany at the end of the First World War? Try to explain your ideas.

Why did hatred of the Jews increase in Germany after 1919?

There were many Jews living in Germany at the time of the First World War. Generally, Jewish people were accepted as part of German society. Even so, some Germans were **anti-Semitic.**

The Treaty of Versailles signed in 1919 (see pages 156–7) blamed Germany for causing the war. Germany had to pay a huge amount of money to repair the war damage in Belgium and France. However, Germany had also suffered from the effects of the war.

The Treaty of Versailles made the German people angry. They wanted someone to blame for their suffering. Jewish businesses had made money during the war while others in Germany had collapsed. Therefore, people blamed the Jews.

The rise of Adolf Hitler and the Nazi Party

In the 1920s, Adolf Hitler became leader of the Nazi Party. Hitler was a good public speaker. He had clear ideas about how to solve Germany's problems and told the German people how he would do this. After 1929, more and more German people began to attend Nazi Party rallies and listen to Hitler's arguments.

Hitler claimed that the German race (Aryan) was superior to all others. It could become a 'master race' but only if it was pure. He said that it had to be free from other, inferior races. Hitler told the German people that Jews were an inferior race.

SOURCE C

Jews will do anything to damage the white race because they hate them. Jewish youths follow innocent young German girls. They lure them away from their own people.

Hitler's anti-Semitic views from his autobiography Mein Kampf ('My Struggle'), written in 1924.

MEMO FROM HITLER

1 Publish only newspapers and books that spread Nazi ideas.
2 Tell Germans to be proud Aryans. Tell them they are better than Jews.
3 Forbid Jews to marry Germans.
4 Jews are no longer German citizens. They have no rights.
5 Boycott Jewish businesses and vandalise their shops.
6 Teachers should pick on Jewish children and humiliate them in front of their classmates.
7 Destroy all Jewish art and books.
8 Jews are no longer allowed to go to university.
9 Jews can be arrested and questioned without explanation.
10 All German children must join a Nazi Youth group to learn about Nazi beliefs.

The Jews are aliens in Germany. In 1933, there were 66,060,000 inhabitants of the German Reich, of whom 499,862 were Jews. What is the percentage of aliens in Germany?

An exercise from a German textbook, 1933.

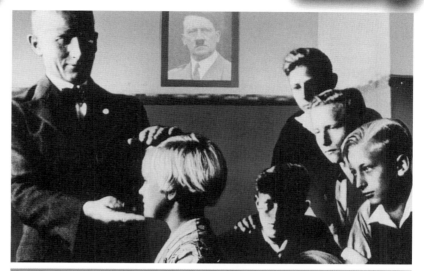

German children being examined for Aryan characteristics — blond hair, blue eyes and physical strength.

A cartoon from a German newspaper in 1935. It shows Jewish butchers making sausages from rats.

HOW DID LIFE CHANGE FOR JEWS LIVING IN EUROPE, 1919–45?

129

TASKS...

1 a) Copy and complete the chart below using Hitler's memo on page 128 and Sources C to F. Give examples to show how Hitler used his power to make life difficult for the Jews.

Area of life which Hitler influenced	How Hitler used his influence to change Jews' lives	How might this change German people's thoughts and actions?
Media		
Education		
Culture		
Economy		
Leisure time		

b) Look at what you have written in the third column in your chart.
   Using two different coloured highlighter pens, mark all the things that you think were:
   • difficult for Jews (one colour)
   • unbearable for the Jews (another colour).
   Don't forget to make a note of your colour code on the chart.

2 Create a mind map to show how the experiences of Jews changed when Hitler came to power. Add points from Sources C to F to the mind map below. You will be able to add more to this as you read on.

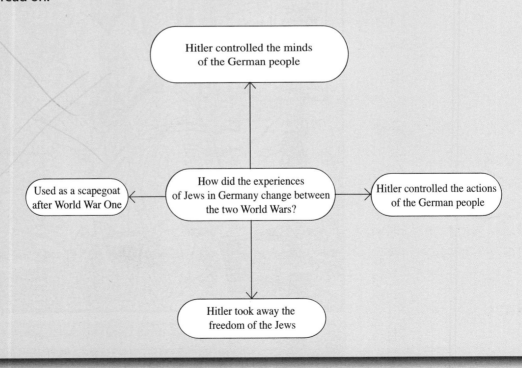

How did Hitler take away the Jews' freedom?

Between 1933 and 1939 Hitler passed laws that made life very difficult for Jews living in Germany (see the timeline below). Some of these laws separated Germany's 500,000 Jews from the rest of the population. Other laws took away their rights. Jews were no longer respected in Germany.

TIMELINE
Anti-Semitism in Germany, 1933–9

1933

30 January: Hitler becomes Chancellor of Germany.

1 April: A boycott of Jewish shops is carried out (a boycott is the refusal to buy goods from a person or persons).

11 May: Hitler's security guard, the SS (*Schutzstaffel*) publicly burn 20,000 books; many are by Jewish authors.

1935

May: Jews are banned from going to public places such as theatres.

15 September: The Nuremberg Laws are passed. These stopped Jews marrying non-Jewish men and women. Jews lost their rights as citizens.

1937

23 July: Jews have to carry identity cards. Their names are changed to 'Israel' and 'Sara' (August)

1938

9/10 October: *Kristallnacht* (Night of Broken Glass) – shop windows are smashed; synagogues are burned; Jews are beaten up.

12 November: Jews can no longer own shops.

16 November: Jewish children have to leave German schools.

3 December: Jews are banned from entering cinemas and the theatre.

1939

Jewish doctors are banned and all Jews lose their jobs.

TASKS...

1 Return to the mind map you started on page 130. Add extra information to show how the German people were encouraged to despise Jews after 1933.

2 Which of the following do you think was most important in changing the lives of Jews in Germany between 1919 and 1933:
   - the Treaty of Versailles
   - the Nuremberg Laws
   - the economic hardship that Germans suffered after 1929.
   - Hitler's book, *Mein Kampf*
   - Hitler's speeches

   Give a reason for your answer.

Plenary

Look at the following three statements.

a) The Jews were used as scapegoats and blamed for Germany's defeat after the First World War.

b) Hitler increased his control over the German people by influencing their minds and actions.

c) The lives of Jews in Germany changed only when Hitler began encouraging people to hate them.

Which of the three statements do you most agree with? Why?

Now write a fourth statement. This will say what the most important factor was in changing the lives of Jews in Germany before 1939.

Key words

Scapegoat Someone who is blamed for other people's problems.

WHAT WAS LIFE LIKE FOR JEWS LIVING IN THE WARSAW GHETTO BETWEEN 1939 AND 1945?

Objectives

In this section you will find out:

- how Jewish people's experiences changed in Europe between 1939 and 1945
- how Jewish people throughout Europe reacted to the changes in their circumstances
- what life was like for Jews living in the Warsaw Ghetto.

To investigate these ideas you will:

- discuss the options available to some Jews
- research the Warsaw Ghetto
- complete a diary to reveal what life was like in the Warsaw Ghetto.

Starter

Look at the cartoon below, which shows a Jewish man considering the options for his family in 1939.

> *We can take the few important things we need and go into hiding.*

> *We can pack up all our things, sell everything and just leave Germany.*

> *We can ignore everything that is going on around us. The Nazis are not going to hurt us. I fought for Germany in the First World War. Surely, things will calm down if we wait.*

With a partner, discuss the advantages and disadvantages of each option.

- *What other questions would you like to ask about each option?*

- *Which option would you take? Why?*

The Warsaw Ghetto

By the early 1940s, Hitler had conquered a large part of Europe. Anti-Jewish policies were enforced in those countries the Nazis conquered. Jews were forced to leave their homes and belongings. They were moved to walled-off areas known as 'ghettos', to separate them from the non-Jewish population in towns and cities. Living conditions in the ghettos were dreadful. There was little sanitation, fresh water, fuel or food, and the overcrowding was unbearable. Thousands died in the ghettos from starvation and from diseases such as **typhus**. Everyone was afraid.

Amazingly, Jews tried to lead a normal life in the ghetto. Children went to school; adults attended lectures and concerts; musicians played and composed; artists painted. Jews also held firmly to their religious beliefs and kept the special religious days – even though this was forbidden. Others formed resistance groups and organised opposition to the Nazis.

Key words

Typhus A highly infectious disease spread by lice.

SOURCE A

Living conditions in the Warsaw Ghetto, 1939.

SOURCE B

The walls around the ghetto cut the Jews off completely from the rest of the world. It prevented Jews from making contact with non-Jews. It left them isolated and suffocated by the overcrowding.

Written by Israel Gutman, who lived in the Warsaw Ghetto.

Children dying of hunger are crying on the street. They howl, beg, sing, moan and shiver with cold. They have no underwear, clothing or shoes. They wrap rags or sacks in strips around their thin bodies. They are already old even though they are only five years old. They are gloomy and weary of life. Hundreds of these children die every day and night. I no longer look when I hear groaning and sobbing. I cross the road.

A description of life in the Warsaw Ghetto by a visitor.

SOURCE D

Queuing for food in the Warsaw Ghetto, 1939.

SOURCE E

There are about 27,000 apartments with an average number of two and a half rooms. About 15 people live in each apartment. Six to seven people live in each room.

The SS officer in charge of the Warsaw Ghetto reported these details to his superior.

SOURCE F

All Jews, the time is coming when you must resist. Not one Jew should go to the railroad cars. If you cannot fight, you can resist by hiding. Our slogan must be, 'All are ready to die as human beings'.

From the public manifesto of a Jewish fighting organisation in Warsaw, autumn 1942.

Key words

Concentration camp A camp where those whom the Nazis disapproved of or opposed were imprisoned.
Extermination camp A camp specially equipped to carry out mass murder.

The Nazis did not intend that the inmates of the ghettos should stay there permanently. Jews were regularly chosen to be deported to **concentration camps** and **extermination camps**. The Jewish resistance groups tried unsuccessfully to stop these deportations. Once all the Jews were removed, the deserted ghettos were 'liquidated' (destroyed).

SOURCE G

Jews in ghettos were determined to survive. They organised themselves into groups. Some worked as couriers, travelling from ghetto to ghetto to pass on information. It was dangerous work. Children often became smugglers, escaping from the ghettos to scavenge for food.

From a modern history book.

Key words

Annihilated Destroyed without trace.

The Warsaw Ghetto, in Poland, is remembered for the courage and defiance of its inmates in resisting the Nazis. More than 400,000 Jews were forced to live in a tiny area of the city. By the time the ghetto was **annihilated** in May 1943, very few had survived.

TASKS...

1 You are going to write a diary account of what life was like in the Warsaw Ghetto. Use Sources A to G to help you make your account realistic. However, before you begin your writing, you need to do some preparation.

a) Copy and fill in the chart below to show what it was like in the Warsaw Ghetto. Use the information from this chapter and Sources A to G to give examples of each of the aspects on the chart.

b) Look over your completed chart. Think carefully about what you have learned. What do you think it might have been like:
- having no food
- living in unhealthy, overcrowded conditions
- always being afraid of being deported
- not knowing where your relatives and friends have been taken
- seeing children and adults dying every day?

Share your thoughts with others in the class.

Aspect of life in Warsaw Ghetto	Evidence
Food	
Education	
Morale	
Religion	
Housing	
Other	

c) Add a third column to the table, 'My thoughts'. In this column put your thoughts into words for each aspect.

WS Now write your diary account of life in the ghetto using your chart. Write in the first person and try to include as much detail as possible.

Plenary

Write down three words that you think best describe life in the Warsaw Ghetto. Explain why you have chosen these words. Compare your words and ideas with the rest of your class.

WHY DID SO FEW PEOPLE SURVIVE THE AUSCHWITZ-BIRKENAU CONCENTRATION CAMP?

Objectives

In this section you will find out:
- how Jewish people's experiences changed in Europe between 1939 and 1945
- what life was like in the Auschwitz-Birkenau concentration camp
- why so few people survived life in the camp.

To investigate these ideas you will:
- study a poem about the camp
- look at evidence about life in the camp.

Starter

Read this poem.

What big heavy doors!
Strange lingering odour,
faint but still here … strong disinfectant.
'Stand round the shower point.'
Wait for the water. Don't think about the crowd.
They don't notice your degredation.
They can't see your shaved head from all the rest!

My God! … They're locking those bloody great doors!
Why? It can't be!
No, the water will come in a minute.
Don't cry, just be patient,
It will be over very soon.

There's a noise – up there.
He's lifting that grate.
All eyes watching, wondering.
No sound.
What are those pellets? Dry disinfectant?
Sulphur!!?

Gas! Gas! Gas! Panic!
The screams, the clutching,
Pulling, scrambling.
The total terror of realisation.

Timeless minutes climbing and scrambling.
Families forgotten. Self-preservation.
Flesh on flesh – clutching and tearing.
Gas, screams, death … silence.

A poem by Elizabeth Wyse from *The Auschwitz Poems.*

Read the poem carefully. What questions does it make you want to ask about the person in the poem?

Hitler's 'Final Solution' to the Jewish problem

After the outbreak of the Second World War, German troops swept across Europe. The countries they occupied had large Jewish populations. Hitler continued his anti-Jewish policies in these countries.

In 1942, it was decided to move European Jews into special camps. Those who were fit would be worked to death. Those who were old and unfit, and young children would be sent immediately to huge gas chambers where they would be killed. The Nazis planned to exterminate eleven million Jews, gypsies and other 'inferior' people. This became known as the 'Final Solution'. Six death camps were built across Europe for this purpose.

Sending Jews to the death camps

Already, Jews in Nazi occupied countries had been forced to move into ghettos. The Jewish committees that ran these ghettos were ordered to provide lists of people to be transported. At first, no one knew where the Jews were going. They were allowed to take one suitcase. They were told they were being 'resettled' more comfortably. At first, people believed this, however, as time went by these regular transports caused great fear.

SOURCE **B**

This photograph shows Jews being taken to a death camp in a crowded freight truck, 1942.

Jews were herded into freight trucks on trains that ran along specially built railway lines. These journeys took several days. Conditions were dreadful – the trucks were overcrowded and there was little sanitation, water or food. Many people were in a very poor state by the time they arrived; some died on the way.

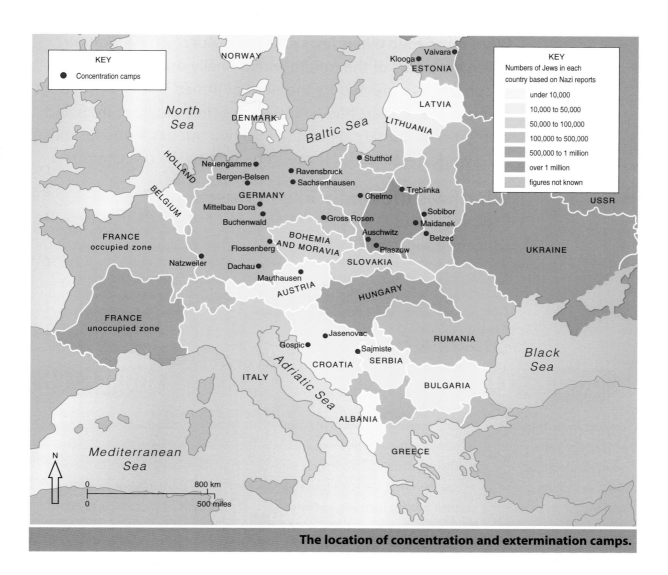

The location of concentration and extermination camps.

HOW DID LIFE CHANGE FOR JEWS LIVING IN EUROPE, 1919–45?

Key words

Slav Natives of some eastern European countries.

We were taken to a train station, put into groups of 60 and crowded into freight trucks. Each of us was given a bucket to use as a toilet. We wondered where we were going and how long the journey would last. It was difficult to see outside because there was only a small window.

An account given by Errikos Sevillias, who was sent to Auschwitz-Birkenau.

The Auschwitz-Birkenau concentration camp

Auschwitz-Birkenau was the largest concentration camp and it has become most closely associated with the Holocaust. 1.5 million people died there. Those who died were mostly Jews but included others that the Nazis hated – **Slavs**, gypsies, Jehovah's Witnesses and homosexuals.

What happened when Jews arrived at Auschwitz-Birkenau?

When the doors of the freight trucks finally opened, the prisoners were greeted by the sight of armed soldiers with dogs. Some of the soldiers had whips. As they left the train, men and women were quickly separated into two queues – one for those fit to work, the other for those to be sent to the gas chambers.

What was life really like in Auschwitz?

Look at Sources D to N about life in the Auschwitz-Birkenau concentration camp.

SOURCE D

In most cases, the new arrivals did not know what awaited them. They were invited to undress for showers. The shower rooms had clothes hooks, benches and so forth. But they were really gas chambers in disguise.

From a modern textbook.

SOURCE E

One evening as I was on my way to visit friends, I noticed a group of women standing round a huge wooden tub. They pushed me away but I saw what they were doing. Tiny fingers were grasping the edge of the tub. In order to save mothers who had secretly given birth, these women were drowning their infants. They told each mother that they knew a place where her child could be put away that was safe. Only in this way could the mothers carry on working, otherwise they were sent straight to the gas chambers.

Claudette Kennedy.

SOURCE F

A drawing of the Auschwitz-Birkenau concentration camp by a Holocaust survivor.

SOURCE G

They punched me until I was in a state of collapse. I was eventually locked into a barrack full of people who had been selected for the gas chambers. Realising the consequences, I was determined to escape and managed to climb out at night through a narrow window with a colleague.

An account by a Holocaust survivor, Victor Greenberg.

SOURCE H

We had to wait in queue for our turn, all of us nervous and terrified and trying to keep out of the way of the German soldiers. I realised that the Germans were separating people into rows – one row to the left and the other to the right. I saw the left-hand row was full of children and old people, and I knew that I must avoid it at all costs.

Arek Hersh describes his experience of arriving at Auschwitz-Birkenau.

SOURCE I

A photograph showing daily life in a concentration camp.

SOURCE J

The selection process on the railway platform at Auschwitz-Birkenau, showing two different queues, summer 1944.

SOURCE K

My twin sister Rachel and I were eleven years old. Both of us cried when we were separated from our mother and brother. Then a woman who had been in Auschwitz for a long time came over to us and said: 'Do not cry children. You see, they are burning your parents.'

Vera Blau describes her experiences at Auschwitz-Birkenau.

SOURCE L

When one woman was ordered to undress completely she threw her shoe in the SS guard's face, grabbed his revolver and shot him in the stomach. After her act of defiance, other women began to strike the SS men at the very entrance of the gas chamber, severely injuring two of them.

Report of Jerzy Tabau, a non-Jewish Polish prisoner at Auschwitz, October 1943.

SOURCE M

A photograph showing prisoners putting a dead body into a cremation oven at a concentration camp.

There were many Jewish doctors living in our section of the camp – women doctors, men doctors, eye doctors, ear doctors. Mengele came to speak to them every day and gave them orders what to do with each twin.

Magda Speigel, survivor of Auschwitz. Josef Mengele was a Nazi doctor. He was fascinated by twins and carried out experiments on them. Many died or were left crippled.

TASKS...

1 a) Copy the chart below.

Statement	Evidence for	Evidence against	Should the statement be changed? If yes, how?
No children survived the selection process.			
No one ever tried to escape from Auschwitz-Birkenau.			
No one knew what was happening at Auschwitz-Birkenau.			
People only died in the gas chambers at Auschwitz-Birkenau.			
Hard manual work was the only type of job that the prisoners at Auschwitz-Birkenau were allowed to do.			

b) Now read Sources D–N and evaluate the statements.

2 Why do you think so few men, women and children survived the Auschwitz-Birkenau concentration camp?

Plenary

You can show only one image to other people so that they can learn about Auschwitz-Birkenau. Which image would you choose from this section and why? Share your opinion with the rest of the class.

HOW SHOULD WE REMEMBER THE HOLOCAUST TODAY?

Objectives

In this section you will find out:
- why it is important to learn about the Holocaust
- how we should remember the Holocaust.

To investigate these ideas you will:
- discuss how books, films and events help us to remember the Holocaust
- write an outline for an assembly to **commemorate** the Holocaust.

Starter

It is not what has happened, but what has been prevented from ever taking place — the sum of all unwritten books, thoughts unthought, or unfelt feelings, of works never accomplished, of lives unlived to their natural end.

Paulina Preis writing in 1969.

💡 *Why do you think it is important to be taught about the Holocaust? Share your ideas with others in your class.*

Key words

Commemorate The act of remembering something, often by a public event.
Genocide Mass killing to exterminate a whole race of people.

What happened to the Jews after liberation?

As the Second World War ended, the camps were freed by either the Russian, United States or British armies. What they found was the horrifying evidence of **genocide**. Thousands of bodies had been thrown into shallow graves. Most of the camp survivors were too weak to speak or move.

Liberation of the camps did not end the Jews' problems. They had seen acts of unimaginable cruelty and lost family and friends. They had been humiliated and abused. They had nowhere to go. The communities in which they had once lived no longer existed.

Female guards at the Bergen-Belsen concentration camp in Germany are made to bury the bodies of those people they helped to kill.

The problems Jews faced

Many Jews found it difficult to talk about their experiences. In any case, no one wanted to hear the stories of horror. The survivors of the camps were in very poor health, both mentally and physically.

Worst still, after all that had happened to them, people in their home towns showed hatred towards them when they returned.

How they overcame these problems

Organisations were set up to help the Jews find lost relatives and enable them to re-build their lives. Many left Europe to start new lives in other countries, for example, the USA or Australia. Others went to Israel, the Jewish homeland that was established in 1948.

Remembering the Holocaust

Approximately six million Jews died during the Holocaust. Of these, 1.5 million were children. A further 5.5 million other people also perished. Those who died and those who survived such horror must be remembered. The Holocaust also has lessons for us today.

Every year, there is a national Holocaust Memorial Day. It is a time to remember the victims of the Holocaust and to think about the prejudice and hatred in the world. What will you remember most about the Holocaust? Why? What do you think are the lessons for the world today?

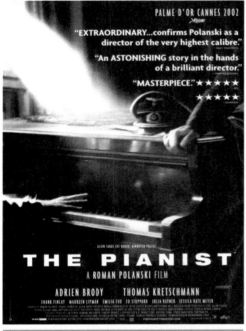

An advertisement for The Pianist, a film about the Holocaust made in 2002.

A Holocaust survivor talking to a group about his experiences.

Yad Vashem Holocaust memorial in Jerusalem, Israel.

TASKS...

1 Look at Sources C to E. How do you think these images help people to remember the Holocaust? Discuss this with a partner.

2 National Holocaust Day in the UK was introduced in 2001. Write a short plan for a school assembly to take place on National Holocaust Day. You may include images and poems if you wish. You must be able to explain why you have included the information you have chosen.

Time	Resource included	Commentary about the resource	Reasons for inclusion

3 Share your assembly ideas with the rest of your class. On which ideas have you agreed and on which have you disagreed? What do you think makes a good assembly?

Plenary

Look back to the facts about the Holocaust on page 125. What three statements would you now like to add to the list?

RIGHTS AND FREEDOMS: CONCLUSION

In this section you have read about people who were deprived of their rights and freedoms. These people are very different. They lived at different times and in different places. You have also looked at the ways in which they tried to win their rights.

Copy this diagram and then look back through the section. Write the groups of people in the middle box. Add the methods of resistance they used in the appropriate box on each side. Draw arrows to link the groups with their actions.

Violence (Active resistance)	The struggle for rights and freedoms – who?	Non-violence (Passive resistance)

Highlight those actions that were most successful.

'Violence never achieves anything.' Work in groups to decide if this is always true, sometimes true or never true. Use the examples you have included in your diagram. Present your ideas to the rest of the class.

THEME: THE CHANGING NATURE OF WARFARE IN THE TWENTIETH CENTURY

INTRODUCTION

In this section you will study events from the three major conflicts of the twentieth century – the First World War, the Second World War and the Cold War. These conflicts changed the world and affected millions of lives in many different ways.

British troops at the Somme, a scene from a British government film, The Battle of the Somme, released in August 1916.

SOURCE B

SOURCE C

The bombing of London during the Second World War, December 1940.

The Berlin Wall, 1962.

WHY DO WARS HAPPEN?

8

DO ALL WARS HAVE THE SAME CAUSES?

Objectives

In this section you will find out:
- why the First World War started
- why tension in Europe was increasing before 1914.

To investigate these ideas you will:
- use information to predict outcomes
- consider the strengths and weaknesses of contemporary accounts.

Starter

Wars happen for many different reasons. In pairs, try to think of at least three reasons why one country might go to war with another. Share your reasons with others in your class. Create a class brainstorm showing all the reasons you have thought of. You will revisit this brainstorm later.

Common causes of war

In the following sections, you will study the causes of the three major wars of the twentieth century:

- the First World War (1914–18)
- the Second World War (1939–45)
- the Cold War (1945–90).

As you study each conflict, look for the common causes of each war. These causes may be linked to the themes below.

Militarism – when countries build up their armies, navies and weapons in order to attack others or defend themselves.

Imperialism – when countries try to build large empires by conquering other countries.

Ideology – a set of beliefs about how a country is governed and how its people are allowed to live.

Alliances – the agreements countries make to support each other, especially during times of war.

Nationalism – the strong feeling of national pride which sometimes makes countries feel superior to others.

WHAT WERE THE CAUSES OF THE FIRST WORLD WAR?

SOURCE A

'I heard that the First World War started when a bloke called Archie Duke shot an ostrich because he was hungry.'

'I think you mean it started when the Archduke of Austria-Hungary got shot.'

'No, there was definitely an ostrich involved.'

'The real reason for the whole thing was that it was too much effort not to have a war.'

A conversation from the BBC comedy series, Blackadder Goes Forth, 1989.

💡 What questions will you need to ask to find out if this comedy history is true?

The First World War (1914–18) was the first major conflict of the twentieth century. Although it began in 1914, the causes of the war go back much further in time. Some go back to the early nineteenth century.

Tensions in Europe before 1914

- Germany was jealous of Britain's empire. The Kaiser (Emperor) wanted an empire as well.

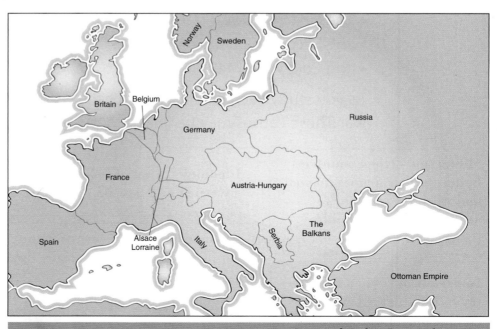

A map showing Europe in 1900.

- In 1839, Britain promised to protect Belgium if it was attacked by Germany.

- In 1871, Germany defeated the French. France wanted revenge for this defeat and its land back.

- In 1882 Germany, Italy and Austria–Hungary formed the Triple Alliance. They promised to help each other if attacked.

- In 1893, France and Russia formed an alliance.

- The Germans knew that they might one day have to fight both France and Russia. So in 1905, they drew up a plan to avoid this – the Schlieffen Plan (see the map below).

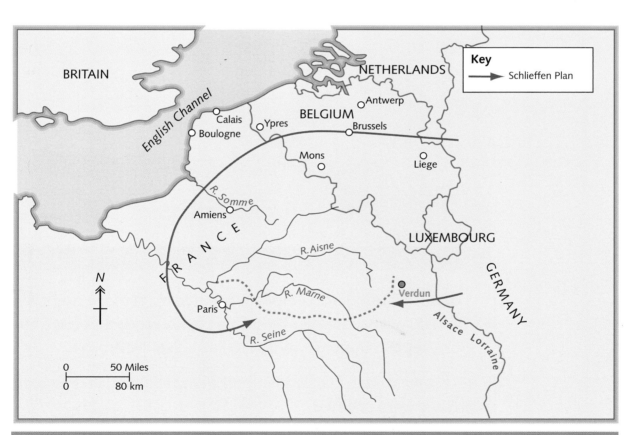

A map showing the route of the Schlieffen Plan.

- The Schlieffen Plan was that Germany would invade France through Belgium (a **neutral** country) and quickly gain control. Then her armies could turn and fight the Russians.

Key words

Neutral Not taking sides.

- In 1906, Britain launched the first *Dreadnought*, the most modern warship of its time. It was quicker and carried bigger guns than other ships.

- In 1907, Germany was proud of its navy. Germans wanted it to be as good as, if not better than, Britain's. So the *Nassau Class* was built to compete with the British *Dreadnought*.

A Dreadnought battleship.

- The Austro-Hungarian Empire was made up of many countries. The different nationalities within the Empire wanted independence. However, the Emperor wanted to keep all of his empire.

- Russia wanted to take land from the Austro–Hungarian Empire, so they were enemies.

- Serbia wanted all Slav people in the Austro–Hungarian Empire to be free and independent. Many Russians were also Slavs, so Russia wanted to help Serbia against Austria–Hungary.

- In 1907 France, Russia and Britain signed an alliance called the Triple Entente, which said they would help each other if attacked.

TASKS...

1 a) Write the heading, *Why wars happen – the long-term causes of the First World War*. Then draw a larger copy of this chart. You read about these themes on page 149.

Themes	Causes
Nationalism	Serbia wanted to unite all Slav people in the Austro-Hungarian Empire.
Militarism	The Schlieffen Plan (1905) was part of Germany's preparation for war.
Imperialism	
Alliances	
Ideology	

b) Now read pages 150–2. Here you will find information about the tensions between the countries in Europe that helped to cause the First World War. Write each of the causes on your chart next to the correct theme. Two of these are completed for you. you might decide that some of the causes belong in more than one box.

2 When you have finished, compare your chart with someone else's to see if they are similar. Explain the decisions you made to the other person.

Short-term causes of the First World War

In 1914, tension in Europe reached its peak. However, the spark that plunged Europe into war was unexpected.

> ### NEWSFLASH!
> 28 June 1914
>
> **Murder in Sarajevo! The Emperor's nephew, Archduke Franz Ferdinand, shot while visiting the capital of Bosnia.**
>
> Archduke Ferdinand and his wife, Countess Sophie, were on an official visit to Sarajevo to inspect the Bosnian Army and to celebrate their wedding anniversary.
>
> In spite of tight security, a Serbian terrorist, Gavrilo Princip, fired two shots into the Archduke's car killing both the prince and his wife. Princip was soon arrested. He belongs to a Serbian terrorist group called the Black Hand. This group wants Bosnia to be free from the Austro-Hungarian Empire.
>
> Austria has blamed the Serbian government for the assassination.

How did the First World War begin?

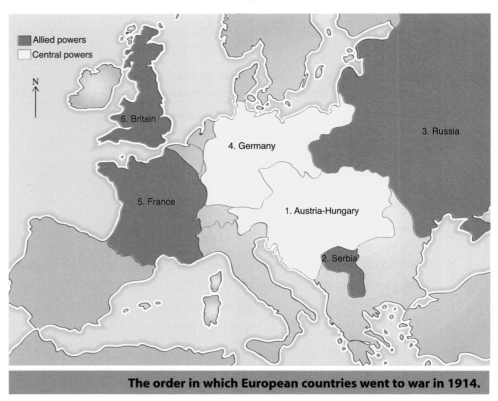

The order in which European countries went to war in 1914.

Allied powers
Central powers

N

6. Britain
3. Russia
4. Germany
5. France
1. Austria-Hungary
2. Serbia

TASKS...

1 Work in pairs or groups and then share your ideas with the rest of the class.

a) The Archduke of Austria has been murdered. What do you think will happen next? Use what you have learned and the map above to help you work out the following:

- If Austria–Hungary attacks Serbia, what will Russia do? Why?
- If Russia threatens Austria–Hungary, what will Germany do? Why?
- If Russia is threatened by Germany, what will France do? Why?
- If Germany has to fight Russia and France, what will it have to do first? Why?
- If Germany marches through Belgium, what will Britain do? Why?

b) Would the First World War have happened had the Archduke not been murdered? Think of as many other reasons as you can why these countries were ready to go to war. (Here are some clues: rivalry, hatred, pride, ambition, arms and armies.)

2 Write a paragraph or draw a flowchart to show why war broke out in 1914.

Plenary

Look back at Source A on page 150. Do you agree with the quote from *Blackadder*? Explain your ideas.

WHAT WERE THE CAUSES OF THE SECOND WORLD WAR?

In this section you will find out:
- how the results of the First World War helped to cause the Second World War
- whether the Second World War could have been avoided
- why the Second World War broke out.

To investigate these ideas you will:
- organise evidence on a mind map
- design a flow chart.

Starter

Some historians have argued that the results of the First World War helped to cause the Second World War. Look back at the map of Europe in 1914 on page 150. Then look at the map below.

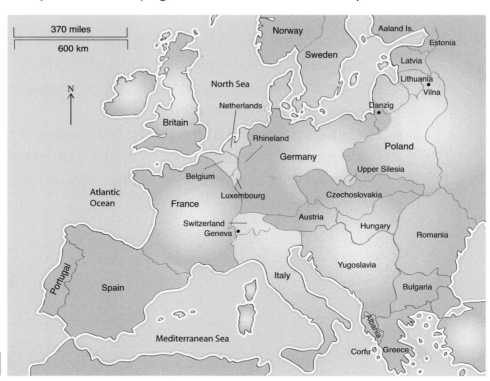

Europe in 1919.

List the differences you notice between Europe in 1914 and Europe in 1919.

💡 Which country do you think would be most upset by the changes that had taken place in Europe by 1919? Explain why.

💡 Can you think of any reasons why this might have led to the Second World War?

The effects of the First World War

On 11 November 1918 at 11 am, the German army surrendered. The First World War was over.

In 1919, the leaders of the victorious nations – Britain, France and the USA – met at the Palace of Versailles in France. They met to discuss the future of Europe. However, their main concern was how to make sure that Germany would not cause another war.

The result of this meeting was a peace settlement called the Treaty of Versailles, which was signed on 28 June 1919. Germany had no say in the terms of the treaty and was punished by its harsh terms. Germany had to:

- accept full blame for starting the First World War
- pay compensation (reparations) of £6600 million for the destruction and damage caused in Belgium and France
- give up its overseas colonies
- give up land in Europe (to make Germany smaller and poorer)
- reduce its military power to an army of 100,000 men and a navy of six battleships; it was not allowed an airforce or submarines.

SOURCE Ⓐ

As a soldier, I cannot help feeling that it were better to perish honourably than accept a disgraceful peace.

Field-Marshal Von Hindenburg, Germany's supreme commander in the First World War, speaking in June 1919.

TASKS...

1 Make a list of adjectives that a German person might use to describe the Treaty of Versailles.
2 Make another list to describe how Germans might feel. How might these feelings have led to a Second World War?

Could the Second World War have been avoided?

The Treaty of Versailles was very unpopular with the German people. Germans felt betrayed by the government for accepting its harsh terms.

SOURCE B

Germans queuing in Hanover to register for unemployment benefit in 1930.

In the post-war years, Germany struggled to pay the reparations it owed. There was widespread poverty, high unemployment and the price of goods rose. The German people did not trust the government to help them. As a result, new political parties that promised an end to the hardship became popular. One of these was the Nazi Party, led by Adolf Hitler. In 1929, there was a terrible worldwide depression (economic crisis). Germany was hit very hard. By 1932, six million German people were unemployed. Many people were hungry and homeless.

The German government had no solutions to these problems, so more and more people began to vote for the Nazi Party. In January 1933, Hitler became the leader of Germany. He promised to make Germany wealthy, powerful and respected again (see Sources C to G).

SOURCE C

'Our last hope: Hitler' – a Nazi poster used in the 1932 election campaign, which targets the unemployed.

WHY DO WARS HAPPEN?

A Nazi election poster of 1928. It says the sacrifices made by Germany in the First World War were in vain

The Nazis promised to make Germany a respected power again and to restore prosperity. These were powerful messages to desperate people.

Hitler was a rousing public speaker. He captivated his audiences. He toured the country delivering speeches to huge audiences. His message was simple. He had something to offer all sections of German society.

A modern historian writing in 2003.

A Nazi election poster of 1932. It says 'Women! Millions of men out of work! Millions of children without a future! Save our German families. Vote for Adolf Hitler!'

Hitler appealed to the whole nation. He declared that Germans deserved to live with pride in a new nation free from the burdens imposed by the Treaty of Versailles. He said that German people were superior and should be protected from those he believed to be inferior such as the Jews.

Hitler had appeal for all classes of people. He promised jobs to the working classes and money to the farmers. German businesses were to be protected from strikes. Hitler was also keen to stress the role that women would play in Nazi Germany. The Nazis wanted to be seen as the party of family values.

Adapted from a modern history textbook.

TASKS...

1 Look at Sources C to G, which describe Hitler's promises to the German people. Sort them into three groups:
   - those that would *not* cause war
   - those that *might* cause war
   - those that *would* definitely cause war.

2 Which promise do you think would have won Hitler the most votes? Explain your answer carefully.

3 Make a chart like the one you filled in for the First World War (see page 153). Now fill in the chart for the Second World War. Decide under which theme each of Hitler's promises should go. Write on your chart only those promises that you think might lead to war. You will add some more information to this chart at the end of this section.

Why did the Second World War break out?

Once Hitler became leader of Germany, he began to act on his promises. This started a sequence of events that led to war in 1939. Some historians believe that Britain and France could have stopped Hitler at an earlier stage. When you have read more, you can decide whether you agree or not.

TASKS...

1 In pairs, imagine you are advisers to the British government between 1933 and 1939. For each of Hitler's actions on pages 160–1, what advice you would give the British government on how to deal with it? You may choose from the suggestions or make up your own advice. Remember to take into account the information in the thought bubbles for each situation.

SITUATION ONE

After becoming leader of Germany in 1933, Hitler begins to re-arm. He increases the army and air force, secretly at first. However, it soon becomes clear to the British government that Germany is re-arming. What action should Britain take?

Three options:
a) Attack Germany and destroy the weapons.
b) Do nothing.
c) Agree new limits with Hitler on the size of his military.

What might the British government think?

Hitler is breaking the terms of the Treaty of Versailles.

Hitler should be stopped before he gets too strong.

Maybe we should allow this. The Soviet Union is a greater threat to us than Nazi Germany. Hitler could help us to fight them, if necessary.

SITUATION TWO

It is 1936. Hitler sends his troops into the Rhineland (see the map on page 155), which had been demilitarised by the Treaty of Versailles. What action should the British government take?

Three options:
a) Send an army to the Rhineland to stop Hitler.
b) Allow Hitler to keep troops there.
c) Let Hitler know that you don't like what he is doing.

What might the British government think?

Hitler has broken the Treaty of Versailles again. Troops cannot enter the Rhineland.

The Rhineland is really German. Perhaps German troops have a right to be there.

The German army is still small. We could stop Hitler now before the army gets any bigger.

SITUATION THREE

It is 1938. Hitler has broken the Treaty of Versailles again. He has sent his troops into Austria and announced his intention to unite Germany with Austria (the *Anschluss*). What action should the British government take?

Three options:
a) Do nothing and allow the Anschluss to continue.
b) Tell Hitler to cancel the Anschluss or risk war.
c) Ask the Austrian government if it wants the Anschluss or not, then make a decision.

What might the British government think?

People in Britain do not want another World War.

Hitler is continuing to ignore the Treaty of Versailles.

Hitler says that he wants peace. Maybe he will stop if Germany is allowed to unite with Austria.

There are lots of German-speaking people in Austria. The Austrian government wants the Anschluss, so why stop it?

SITUATION FOUR

It is September 1938. Hitler has demanded that the Sudetenland (see the map on page 155) be returned to Germany. (The Sudetenland is an area in eastern Czechoslovakia.) What should the British government do?

Three options:

a) Ask the Czech government what they want and then decide what to do.

b) Allow Hitler to have the Sudetenland, although he must agree to leave the rest of Czechoslovakia alone.

c) Declare war on Germany.

What might the British government think?

Most of the people in the Sudetenland are German speaking and want to reunite with Germany.

The Czech government is worried that Hitler will take the rest of Czechoslovakia.

The British people do not want to go to war with Germany.

Hitler is continuing to break the Treaty of Versailles.

SITUATION FIVE

It is March 1939. Hitler's troops have invaded the rest of Czechoslovakia. What action should the British government take?

Three options:

a) Do nothing to help Czechoslovakia.

b) Declare war on Germany to help the Czechs.

c) Threaten Hitler with war if he invades another country (you think he might invade Poland next).

What might the British government think?

Britain and France need more time to prepare for war against Hitler.

Hitler has broken all his promises and must be stopped!

Czechoslovakia needs help. It cannot fight Hitler alone.

SITUATION SIX

It is the 1 September 1939. Hitler has invaded Poland to take land taken from Germany in the Treaty of Versailles. What should the British government do?

Two options:

a) Do nothing, and hope that Hitler will stop invading other countries.

b) Declare war on Germany. (Britain has already promised to help Poland if attacked.)

What might the British government think?

Hitler seems to be trying to take over Europe. He must be stopped.

Hitler's promises mean nothing. He clearly does not want peace and force is the only way to stop him.

Hitler is just trying to take back what he feels belongs to Germany. We might as well cancel the Treaty of Versailles.

What did Britain do?

The British and French governments wanted to avoid another war so they followed a policy called appeasement. They agreed to give in to Hitler's demands on the condition that he agreed to guarantee peace. In this way, they hoped to prevent war. The British people supported appeasement because many families lost loved ones in the First World War. However, appeasement failed to keep peace because Hitler never kept any of his promises.

TASKS...

1 a) Draw a flow chart like the one below, to summarise the road to war between 1933 and 1939. On the flow chart, you should show the actions Hitler took and the reactions of the allies.

Hitlers actions	The path to war	The Allies' reactions
←	**1933**	→
←	**1936**	→
←	**1938**	→
←	**1939**	→

b) Do you think that the Second World War could have been avoided? Look at your flow chart. Highlight the points at which you think Hitler could have been stopped.

c) Share your thoughts with the class. Do you all agree? You could hold a class discussion or debate on this question.

2 Look back to your Second World War chart completed on page 159. Add details about the causes from pages 160–1 that match the themes on the chart.

3 Now look at your completed 'themes' charts for the First and Second World Wars. Can you see any links or similarities between the causes of both wars

Plenary

Was Hitler, the Treaty of Versailles or the policy of appeasement really to blame for the outbreak of the Second World War? Explain your answer carefully.

WHAT WERE THE CAUSES OF THE COLD WAR?

Objectives

In this section you will find out:
- why the USA and the Soviet Union became enemies after 1945
- how the results of the Second World War helped to cause the Cold War.

To investigate these ideas you will:
- classify information to show the differences between communism and capitalism
- prepare two radio reports and complete a mind map.

Starter
Look at Source A.

Damage at Hiroshima after the explosion of an atomic bomb on 6 August 1945.

Source A shows the destruction of a Japanese city, Hiroshima, by a US nuclear bomb at the end of the Second World War.

What effect do you think that scenes like this had on people in 1945? How have nuclear weapons changed our views about future wars? Discuss this with a partner and then your class.

What was the cold war?

By the time the Second World War ended, the USA and the Soviet Union were the strongest nations in the world. They became known as 'superpowers'. They were also enemies. The conflict between them was known as the Cold War.

The conflict between the superpowers was described as a 'cold' war because of the suspicion and hostility that existed between them. It did not result in actual fighting because by 1950, both the USA and the Soviet Union had nuclear weapons. This meant that if fighting broke out it would result in total destruction for both sides. Therefore a war of words, **propaganda** and threats developed.

Why were the USA and the Soviet Union enemies after 1945?

The USA and the Soviet Union were enemies because they had different ideas about how a country is governed.

Key words

Propaganda Information used to persuade people to believe a particular point of view.
Capitalism Freedom for individuals to invest money (capital), make a profit and become rich.
Communists People who believe that the divisions between rich and poor should be removed so that all property, businesses, industry and land belong to the state and not individuals.

The United States of America

The USA was a **capitalist** country that believed in:

- choice of a number of political parties
- democracy, all adults have the right to vote
- freedom of individuals to own businesses and homes
- freedom of individuals to become wealthy
- freedom of individuals to be responsible for themselves without government interference.

The Soviet Union

The Soviet Union was a **communist** country that believed in:

- government by one political party
- a kind of democracy – adults could vote but only for the Communist Party
- State (government) ownership of all business and property
- an equal society – profits are used for the good of all people. No individual freedom.

TASKS...

1 John lives in capitalist USA and Alexander lives in the communist Soviet Union. Below are some statements made by either John or Alexander about their life. Decide who would have said which statement.

Capitalist John

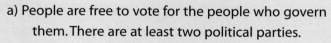

a) People are free to vote for the people who govern them. There are at least two political parties.

b) I work hard, like everyone else, for my country not for myself. People are only free when they are equal.

c) I need special permission to travel abroad. The government uses its money to provide holidays for the people.

d) I own my own shop. I am able to make a profit.

e) I can find out from the newspapers if the government has done anything wrong.

f) People can vote for the one political party that will truly take care of their interests.

g) The state owns all businesses. People work hard to make the country richer.

h) The government owns the newspapers and radio. These tell me what the government is doing well.

i) I own my house. I am free to sell it whenever I want and move to a different part of the country.

j) I work hard to make money for myself. People should be free to earn as much money as they can make through their own efforts.

k) Under our system there is no private ownership of property. The government owns all property.

l) I can go on holiday whenever I like and wherever I like.

Communist Alexander

2 What do you think John would have thought of Alexander's way of life? In pairs, jot down some ideas.

3 What do you think Alexander would have thought of John's way of life? In pairs, jot down some ideas.

4 Which way of life do you prefer? Why?

How did the Cold War start?

The expansion of communism

During the Second World War, the Soviet Union and the USA had been allies. However, they did not trust each other. The USA was bitterly opposed to communism. It feared that the Soviet Union was trying to spread communism across the world. Most Soviet politicians, however, felt threatened from the capitalist countries of western Europe, especially Britain and France.

Between 1945 and 1948, Stalin (the Soviet President) made sure that every country in Eastern Europe had a Communist government that would obey the Soviet Union. This protected the Soviet Union from the West.

The spread of communism in Eastern Europe after the Second World War.

Land taken by Soviet Union at the end of Second World War

Soviet-controlled communist countries

Non-Soviet-controlled communist country

250 miles
400 km

💡 Look at the map. Do you think that the actions of the Soviet Union would make the situation better or worse? Why?

The 'iron curtain'

Capitalist countries in the West were alarmed by the spread of communism into Eastern Europe. They believed that freedom, democracy and the capitalist way of life were under threat. They were determined to stop communism from spreading any further.

In March 1946, the British Prime Minister, Winston Churchill, talked about an 'iron curtain' coming down across Europe. Europe had been divided in half, he said – with capitalist countries to the west and communist countries to the east. Behind the 'iron curtain', people were not free and had to do what their government dictated.

SOURCE B

PEEP UNDER THE IRON CURTAIN

A cartoon published in the Daily Mail in March 1946, commenting on Churchill's 'iron curtain' speech.

💡 What do you think the Soviet Union would have thought of Winston Churchill's 'iron curtain' speech?

TASKS...

1 Look at Source B. What do you think the cartoonist is saying about Churchill's speech?
2 Draw another chart like the ones you did for the First and Second World Wars (see pages 153 and 159). Add the causes of the Cold War that you have discovered so far under the appropriate themes on the diagram.

How real was the threat of nuclear war during the Cold War?

TIMELINE
The arms race, 1945–60

1945 6 August: the USA drops the first ever **atomic bomb** on Hiroshima in Japan, causing mass destruction.

1949 The Soviet Union successfully tests its own atomic bomb.

1952 The USA develops the **hydrogen bomb** (H–bomb).

1953 The Soviet Union develops a hydrogen bomb.

1955 The Soviet Union develops its own submarine-launched nuclear missiles.

1957 The Soviet Union begins developing **nuclear missiles** that can hit targets thousands of miles away.

1958 The USA begins development of long-range missiles.

1960 A US submarine launches a long-range missile from underneath the sea.

1960 Both the USA and the Soviet Union have enough nuclear weapons to destroy the population of the earth. Some believed that this made war less likely – there would be no winners! These weapons are called **nuclear deterrents.**

Key words

Atomic bomb A bomb in which atoms are split releasing tremendous energy.
Hydrogen bomb A bomb, more powerful than the atom bomb, that releases energy from hydrogen atoms.
Nuclear missiles Any bomb that releases tremendous energy from atoms.
Nuclear deterrents Weapons that discourage war for fear of the consequences.

TASKS...

1 **a)** What does the timeline tell you about another cause of tension between the two superpowers?
   b) Add this cause to your Cold War chart in the correct place.

2 Do you agree that if all countries have nuclear weapons no one will dare to use them? Explain your answer. Think about recent world events and terrorist activities and what could happen.

How did the results of the Second World War help to cause the Cold War?

In February 1945, before the end of the Second World War, the allies met at Yalta in the Soviet Union. Prime Minister Churchill of Britain, President Roosevelt of the USA and Stalin, the leader of the Soviet Union, met to plan the final defeat of Germany and to decide what would happen afterwards. They agreed that Germany had to be kept weak, so they decided to split Germany into four zones. Each zone would be controlled by Britain, France, the USA and the Soviet Union. The capital city of Germany, Berlin, fell into the Soviet zone, so Berlin was also split into four zones. East Berlin would be controlled by the Soviet Union.

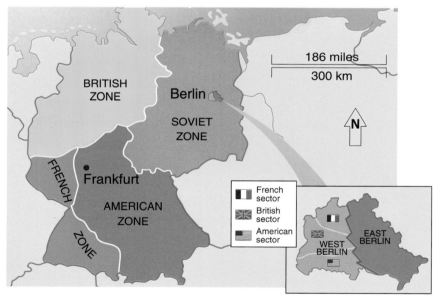

The division of Germany in 1945.

💡 How do you think Berliners might have felt about their city being divided up in this way? What sort of things could happen to families and friends?

By 1948 Britain, France and the USA had changed their minds about Germany. They wanted Germany to be strong so that it would block the spread of communism from the east. They decided to work together to help Germany become rich again. Joseph Stalin was angry about this and took action.

The Berlin Blockade

On 24 June 1948, Soviet troops cut off all land links between West Germany and West Berlin. The plan was to starve West Berliners into accepting communist rule. Britain, France and the USA had to think carefully about what to do next.

- They could stand up to the Soviet Union and risk another war, but no-one wanted another war.
- They could let the Soviet Union take Berlin, but this would help the spread of communism.
- The Soviets could not cut off airways to Berlin, so they could foil Stalin's plans by flying food into West Berlin.
- The USA could quietly threaten Stalin by basing US B-29 bombers in Britain (the same ones that dropped the bomb on Hiroshima!).

THE BIRD WATCHER

A Punch cartoon of July 1948 about the Berlin Blockade, entitled 'The Bird Watcher'. The man holding the gun is Stalin.

💡 What would you advise the Western powers to do? Share your ideas with the rest of the class, giving reasons for your decision.

The Allies dealt with the blockade by airlifting food and supplies into Berlin.

The Berlin airlift

Between July 1948 and May 1949, 1.5 million tonnes of food and supplies were flown into West Berlin by the Western powers. The airlift was expensive, difficult and dangerous. There was always a risk that Soviet planes in the area might attack. About 79 crew members were killed, but in the end the airlift worked! On 12 May 1949, Stalin ended the blockade.

TASKS...

1 It is 12 May 1949 and the Berlin Blockade has ended.

a) In groups, prepare a radio report for British radio about the Berlin crisis. It will include interviews with key people.

- First look back over what you have read about the crisis.
- Then choose the 'characters' for your report e.g. a reporter, a Berliner, an American or British pilot, a Soviet spokesperson and any others.
- The reporter will have to set the scene by telling listeners what has been happening in Germany since the end of the Second World War and why the crisis has happened.
- As a group, work out what interview questions the reporter will need to ask.
- The 'characters' will need to work out their answers. Remember that the Soviet spokesperson will have a different view from the rest!
- Try to use words such as *illegal, unjust, underhand, justified, clever* to describe Stalin's blockade. Use words such as *heroic, brave, life-saving* to describe the airlift (you can work out which characters would use these words!) Add words of your own.
- You need to make the programme flow so try to include words like *later, meanwhile, because, however*.

b) When you have finished your broadcasts, present them to others in the class. Compare each broadcast and decide which was the most successful and why.

2 Draw a mind map or time chart to show how the results of the Second World War contributed to the Cold War.

NATO and the Warsaw Pact

As a result of the Berlin Blockade, the western countries wanted to protect themselves against the Soviet Union. So, in 1949, the North Atlantic Treaty Organisation (NATO) was formed. In 1955, West Germany joined NATO. The Soviet Union felt threatened by NATO and set up its own military alliance, the Warsaw Pact.

Members of NATO

The USA, Britain, Belgium, Canada, Denmark, France, Greece, Iceland, Italy, Luxembourg, the Netherlands, Norway, Portugal, Turkey, West Germany.

Members of the Warsaw Pact

The Soviet Union, Albania, Bulgaria, Czechoslovakia, East Germany, Hungary, Poland, Romania.

A map showing NATO and the Warsaw Pact.

TASKS...

1 Why do you think the existence of NATO and the Warsaw Pact was so dangerous? Think back to what happened in 1914.

2 Go back to the chart you started on page 167. Add any further details you have discovered about the causes of Cold War.

3 Your charts should now be complete for the each of the three wars covered in this chapter. Look at them carefully. Choose the information from the charts that will support the following statements:

   • Wars in the twentieth century have similar causes.

   • There are some differences in the cause of the wars we have studied.

Plenary

Work in pairs or groups. What are the most important points you have learned about why wars happen? Explain your answer. Share your ideas with other groups. How do you think future wars could be avoided?

HOW AND WHY DID TWENTIETH CENTURY WARFARE CHANGE?

The twentieth century brought a dramatic change in methods of fighting. New technology produced deadlier weapons and new battle tactics. As a result, wars destroyed many more lives and caused much greater damage. They affected millions of people worldwide.

In this chapter, you will compare methods of fighting in three twentieth century wars:

- the First World War   • the Second World War   • the Cold War.

As you study some of the major battles and events of these wars, you will find the answer to the question 'How and why did twentieth century warfare change?'

WHAT HAPPENED DURING THE BATTLE OF THE SOMME?

Objectives

In this section you will find out:
- why 1 July 1916 was such a disaster
- whether the Battle of the Somme was a complete failure to the British army.

To investigate these ideas you will:
- listen to and select details from a story
- show how some effects were more successful than others
- begin a comparison chart.

Starter

Read Sources A, B and C, which give different people's opinions about the preparations for the Battle of the Somme and the first day of battle (1 July 1916).

SOURCE A

Key words

Artillery Large guns.

How did the planners imagine that British soldiers would get through the barbed wire? Who told them that **artillery** fire would pound such wire to pieces? Any soldier could have told them that this lifts wire up and drops it down, often more tangled than before.

Private George Coppard, a survivor of the Battle of the Somme.

The men are in splendid spirits. Several have said that they have never been so well informed about the coming battle. The barbed wire has never been so well cut nor the artillery preparation so thorough. All the commanders are full of confidence.

An extract from the diary of Douglas Haig, the British Commander-in-Chief, dated 30 June 1916.

'Come on, we are ready for you.' Words written by German soldiers before the battle. They appeared on placards above their **trenches**.

Reported in The British Campaign in France and Flanders 1916, by Sir Arthur Conan Doyle.

Key words

Trenches The protective ditches from which soldiers fought the enemy.

💡 *What is different about Sources A and B? Why are they different?*

What was the Battle of the Somme about?

By 1916, the First World War had become a stalemate – neither one side nor the other was winning. The conditions for soldiers fighting in the trenches grew worse. The Battle of the Somme was planned to try to bring victory to Britain and its allies (the armies of Britain, France and Belgium).

TASKS...

1 Below is the story of what happened on 1 July 1916 – the first, disastrous day of the Battle of the Somme. Get into groups of three. As you read the story, you are going to look for reasons for this disaster:
   - one of you should look for examples of poor leadership and planning
   - one of you should look for examples of failing weapons
   - one of you should look for problems that were beyond British control.

What happened on 1 July 1916?
Britain alone
The British launched an attack in the Somme, an area of northern France. This was planned as the battle that would defeat Germany and end the First World War. It should have been a joint British–French attack. However, by 1916, the French were struggling to defend the French fortress town of Verdun, against the Germans. Verdun was the scene of fierce fighting by the French army to prevent the Germans breaking through and

capturing Paris. This meant that the British, under the command of Sir Douglas Haig, attacked alone.

Haig's plan

The German trenches were to be bombarded for a week before the battle. It was thought that this would destroy trenches, machine guns and artillery and kill soldiers. The British troops would then walk in straight lines across **No Man's Land** and take over the German trenches.

Disaster on the Somme!

The plan went terribly wrong! The Germans could see what the British were planning from their position on higher ground, so they built a third line of trenches behind the front line. This strengthened their defences. British **reconnaissance** aircraft could see this, but Haig ignored their reports and warnings.

Unknown to the British, the Germans had also built **bunkers** deep underground. These gave protection to German soldiers and their weapons during the bombardment.

About 1.75 million shells were fired at the German positions in a massive bombardment. The German **front line** trenches were almost totally destroyed. However, one-third of the **shells** were duds and did not explode. So the Germans' new trenches remained intact and their troops were safe underground. The shells also failed to cut the huge belts of barbed wire in between the British and German trenches.

At 7.25 am on 1 July 1916, the British guns stopped firing. 100,000 young and inexperienced soldiers waited in their front line trenches for the order to advance. They expected their task to be easy. They believed that all the Germans would be dead. They were going to become heroes!

At 7.30 am, the whistle blew, signalling the order to climb out of the trenches and attack the enemy

Key words

Battalion A group of soldiers.
No Man's Land The land between enemy trenches.
Reconnaissance To survey an area before battle.
Bunker An underground bomb-proof shelter.
Front line The nearest point to the enemy which suffered the heaviest fighting.
Shells Explosives fired from large guns.

position – to go 'over the top'. The first line of men began to climb through the gaps in the barbed wire into No Man's Land. Suddenly, the Germans opened fire, aiming at the gaps in the barbed wire. Many British soldiers were killed even before they got out of their trenches. The advance continued all day. By the end, 57,000 soldiers had been injured and 20,000 killed. Most of these deaths occurred in the first twenty minutes of the battle.

What had gone wrong?

At 7.25 am, when the German soldiers heard the British guns become quiet, they quickly moved into the front line trench. When the British soldiers appeared, they were ready for them! Casualties were also high because the British soldiers had been ordered to walk over No Man's Land in broad daylight. None of the battle's objectives had been achieved.

British troops going 'over the top' on the first day of the Somme, 1 July 1916.

The machine gun is a much over-rated weapon. Two per **battalion** is enough.

Field Marshall Douglas Haig speaking in 1915.

	Officers	Soldiers
Killed / died of wounds	993	18247
Wounded	1337	34156
Missing	96	2056
Taken prisoner	12	573
Total	**2438**	**55032**

British losses on the first day of the Battle of the Somme.

TASKS...

1. Before you read the story, you were asked to look for the reasons for disaster in one particular area. Write down in your book all the reasons you can remember.

2. Get back into your group. Between you, copy and complete the chart below to show why the Battle of the Somme was such a disaster.

Examples of poor leadership and planning	Examples of failing technology	Examples of things beyond British control

3. Look carefully at your completed chart. Are there any reasons that could be put under more than one heading? Shade these on your chart.

Was the Battle of the Somme a complete failure?

The Battle of the Somme continued until November 1916. By that time, more than one million men had become casualties. Was it worth the sacrifice? The map and Sources G to L will help you to decide whether the results of the battle were worth all the injuries and deaths.

SOURCE G

Ten of the tanks were hit by German artillery fire, nine broke down with mechanical difficulties and five failed to move. But recognising their potential, Haig had asked for 1000 more tanks to be built. The Germans were far behind in their tank experiments.

A modern historian writes about what happened at the Somme in September 1916, when 45 British tanks went into battle for the first time.

SOURCE H

British	420,000
French	200,000
German	650,000

The casualty figures for the Battle of the Somme, 1916.

SOURCE J

SOURCE I

The Somme is the muddy grave of the German army.

Spoken by German General Paul von Hindenburg.

British troops at the Battle of the Somme in October 1916.

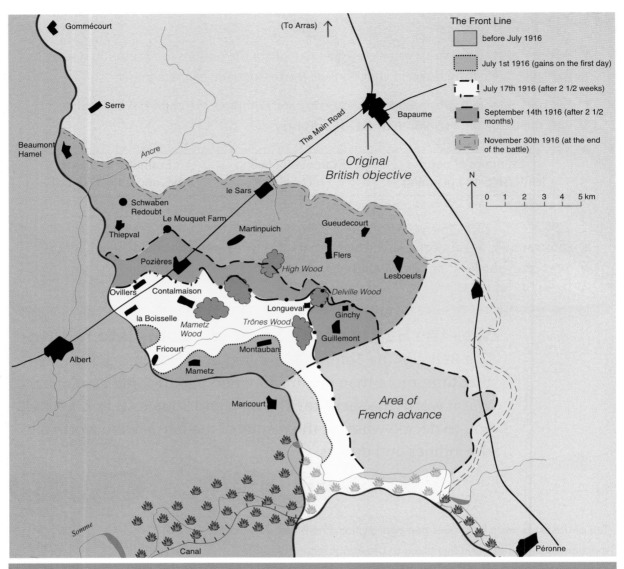

The Somme battlefield, July to November 1916. The battle ended in stalemate.

We are slowly but surely killing off the best of the male population of these islands. Can we afford to go on paying this high price for such little gain?

A letter written by the politician Lord Lansdowne to the Daily Telegraph, 29 November 1916.

Key words

Infantry Soldiers that fight on foot.

The strength and power of the British attack on 1 July 1916 resulted in the Germans moving 60 heavy guns and two **infantry** divisions from Verdun to the Somme. This put an end to the German hopes of victory at Verdun.

A modern historian writing in 1994.

TASKS...

1 Study the map on page 178 and Sources G to L. They all give you ideas about whether the Battle of the Somme was a success or a failure.

   a) In your book, copy and complete the success/failure line below. Select the important point from each source and the map, and note it in your own words in the appropriate place along the line. Where you position each point depends on how strongly you think it proves the Battle of the Somme was a success or a failure.

   Success ◄──────────────────────────────► **Failure**

   b) Discuss your ideas with a partner to see if you agree on where each point should be placed.

2 Now use your success/failure line to write a paragraph summarising your answer to the question: *'Was the Battle of the Somme a complete failure?'*

3 Draw a large copy of the comparison chart below. Write on it what you have learned about the Battle of the Somme under the headings on the chart. You will add more to this chart as you work through the chapter.

Conflict	Main weapons	Tactics used	Who won?
First World War: Battle of the Somme			

The East Surrey Regiment kicking a football across No Man's Land, July 1916.

SOURCE M

Plenary

Look at Source M. This picture was shown to the British public as an image of the Battle of the Somme.

💡 Does Source J give us an accurate impression of the battle? Explain your ideas.

💡 Why do you think the government wanted to show images like this to the British public?

WHY DID FRANCE FALL IN 1940?

In this section you will find out:
- why the German army conquered France so easily in 1940
- how far weapons and tactics had changed by 1940.

To investigate these ideas you will:
- create a plan of attack
- study the use of propaganda.

Starter

Look at the following map, which shows the position of French and British troops and defences to stop Germany invading France.

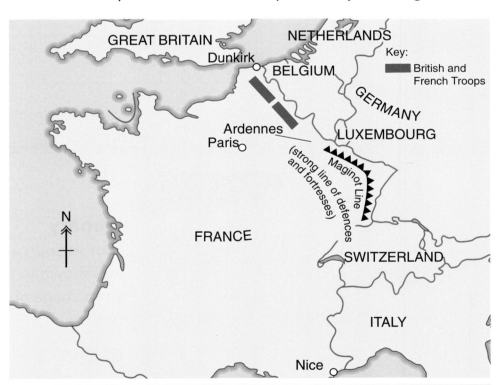

A map giving information to help you plan an invasion of France.

You are a German officer planning an attack on France. Use the map to decide if you will attack (a) through Belgium and Holland (b) directly into eastern France or (c) by using a combination of tactics. Work in pairs to devise a plan of attack.

How did the Germans trick the Allied Forces?

After the First World War, the French were determined that they would never be invaded again by Germany. Therefore, in 1930, they began building the Maginot Line (see the map on page 180).

(see the map on page 180)

Key words

Fortress A defensive building.

The Maginot Line was a line of strong **fortresses** about 145 kilometres long. It stretched along the French–German border. The French believed it could not be crossed. They also believed that the German army would be unable to move tanks and equipment through the thick forests to the north of the line. The French and the British were very confident of this so they placed most of their troops along the French–Belgian border (see the map on page 180). They expected the Germans to attack there, as they had done in 1914.

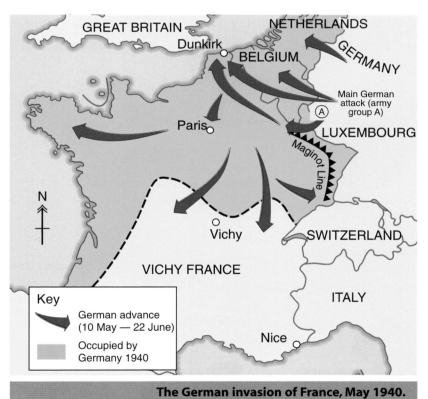

The German invasion of France, May 1940.

On 10 May 1940, the German army *did* launch an attack through Belgium and Holland. The Allies quickly sent troops to deal with it. However, this was a clever trick by the Germans. The attack drew attention away from the main point of the German invasion (see army group A on the map). This attack came through the Ardennes Forest. The real invasion plan starts here.

💡 Look back at the plan of attack which you drew for the Starter activity on page 180. How does it compare with the plan of attack carried out by a real German commander?

How did the Germans conquer France so easily?

The German army advanced rapidly into France in May 1940. Three weeks later, British troops had been forced out. By 22 June the conquest of France was complete.

The Germans had successfully used a new tactic called *Blitzkrieg* (lightning war). *Blitzkrieg* relied mainly on the speed and surprise of the attack. Panzer (tank) divisions were created for the purpose. The attacks consisted of planes, tanks, infantry and artillery that worked together to defeat the enemy. This was made possible by the radio, which allowed effective communication from the commander.

The Allies were slow to react to the *Blitzkrieg*. Their counter-attacks failed because they were disorganised and because British tanks were slow and poorly armed. British tanks were still being used to support the infantry rather than to lead them like the German tanks. This meant that the Allies had to retreat.

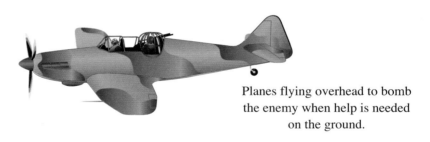

Planes flying overhead to bomb the enemy when help is needed on the ground.

Fast-moving scouts on motorbikes to find the enemy positions.

Tanks to destroy enemy tanks and positions, so that the rest of the army can follow.

Infantry in lorries so that they can keep up with the tanks and help when the fighting is fierce.

The Commander leads his men using the radio to communicate with them all.

How German Panzer divisions worked.

SOURCE A

The tank engine is your weapon as much as its gun.

Spoken by Field Marshall Guderian, the creator and leader of Germany's Panzer divisions.

SOURCE B

Blitzkrieg depended on planes, tanks, infantry and artillery working together. In this respect, radiotelephony – use of the radio to communicate – was the most important part of this new style of war.

A modern historian writing about *Blitzkrieg*.

TASKS...

1 Read Source A. Why was the engine of the tank so important?
2 Look back at the information on page 182 and read Source B. Make a list of the reasons why *Blitzkrieg* was so successful.

Was the evacuation of Dunkirk a German victory?

By 27 May 1940, the Allied Forces had retreated to the Channel port of Dunkirk on the French coast (see the map on page 180). They were surrounded by the German army. A huge rescue effort was mounted from Britain to bring the troops home. But as they waited on the beaches, the German *Luftwaffe* (air force) bombed them.

TASKS...

1 Look at the two accounts below. They show how the evacuation of Dunkirk might have been portrayed in a British and a German newspaper in 1940.
   What do you think the newspaper articles agree on?

Unbeatable! – tens of thousands safely home

Under heavy enemy fire, ships of all sizes have bravely brought our troops back to England from Dunkirk. Many heroes have helped to create this miracle. They have brought their little boats from far and wide to sail alongside our great navy to bring our army home. The men have returned gloriously and in high spirits. They are keen to go back soon and beat the Germans once and for all.

Victory! – British army pushed off French soil

One of the most powerful armies in the world has been forced to flee from Dunkirk. The power and speed of our advance overwhelmed the Allied Forces. Our magnificent *Luftwaffe* has made the evacuation miserable for them. In their hurry to escape, they left most of their equipment and many prisoners. Our conquest of France is complete.

TASKS...

2 Both of the articles on page 183 are propaganda – articles that try to persuade people to believe one point of view. Each side is claiming victory. Pick out three words or phrases from each article that have been used to make you believe that side won. Draw a chart like the one below. Put the words you have chosen into the British or German columns. Two examples are on it already.

British propaganda	Neutral	German propaganda
Unbeatable		*Victory*

3 Look at the statements below. Each contains facts about Dunkirk. Which of these statements do you think support the British account and which support the German account? Add them to your chart by writing the number of each fact in the correct column. Some facts do not support either viewpoint: add these numbers to the neutral column.

1 Nearly 340,000 British and Allied troops were evacuated between 27 May and 4 June 1940. The government had hoped to rescue about 50,000.

2 After Dunkirk, the Germans completed the conquest of France. On 22 June 1940, the French surrendered and signed a peace agreement with Adolf Hitler.

3 In the evacuation, the British left behind most of their heavy military equipment — 75,000 vehicles, 2500 anti-aircraft guns and 11,000 machine guns. These fell into the hands of the Germans.

4 The *Luftwaffe's* bombing of the beaches was not very successful because the sand absorbed the explosive shock. There were few casualties.

5 The Royal Navy worked hard to get men aboard as calmly as possible. Eyewitnesses praised them for this.

6 More than 68,000 British soldiers were killed, wounded, captured or missing.

8 By saving the British Expeditionary Force (BEF), the British government had kept its professional army alive. It would be able to fight in future campaigns and train new recruits.

7 The Royal Air Force (RAF) did little to support the evacuation of Dunkirk, allowing the *Luftwaffe* to bomb the ships and beaches. The RAF was later criticised for this by Dunkirk survivors.

9 Only 26,500 of the 340,000 troops were rescued by civilian boats.

4 Use the information on your chart to write an unbiased newspaper report about what happened at Dunkirk – that is, a report that supports neither one side nor the other.

Carefully explain the points that you make and support your report with evidence.

- You need a headline (no more than six words) that tells readers about the evacuation.

- Use only the facts from your chart to describe what happened. Write about the events in the order in which they happened. Try to use words to join up the parts of your account such as *firstly, secondly, meanwhile, later, because, next, however, although*.

- You should explain how the troops came to be on the beaches of Dunkirk and why they needed to be evacuated.

- Explain that both the British and the German armies are claiming victory and say why.

- Finish your article by giving a balanced view as to the outcome of Dunkirk – did the Germans or the British win or lose, or did neither side win? Try to use words that show you are trying to be fair such as *on the one hand, on the other hand, on balance*.

Plenary

Look back to your comparison chart, which you began on page 179.

Add a second row about the fall of France in the Second World War (as below), then fill in the details.

Conflict	Main weapons	Tactics used	Who won?
First World War: Battle of the Somme			
Second World War: the fall of France			

This chart is still not complete, so make sure there is enough space for one more comparison, which will come at the end of the chapter.

WHAT HAPPENED DURING THE CUBAN MISSILE CRISIS?

Objectives

In this section you will find out:
- how close nuclear war was in 1962
- who 'won' the Cuban Missile Crisis.

To investigate these ideas you will:
- analyse sources
- examine a timeline.

Starter

Study the map below, then answer the questions that follow.

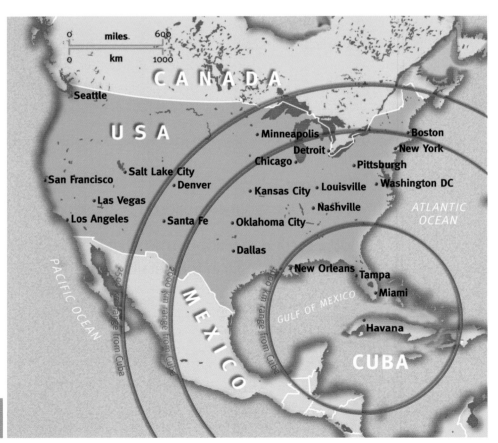

The United States and Cuba.

💡 *Think of three questions you would like to ask to find out more about this map. Write these questions down.*

What was the Cold War about?

During the Second World War, the USA and the USSR (Soviet Union) worked together to defeat Hitler. After the war ended in 1945, they grew suspicious of each other. This was because the USSR was a communist country and the USA was a capitalist country. Each saw the other as a threat. This period of rivalry and suspicion was known as the Cold War. It was a war of words and threats instead of fighting.

Nuclear weapons

The hostility grew worse in 1949 when the USSR developed a nuclear bomb. (The USA had already done this in 1945.) The two countries began to compete to develop more powerful nuclear weapons and longer-range missiles. By the 1960s, both countries had enough nuclear weapons to destroy the world several times over.

💡 Does this new information help you to answer any of your questions from page 186?

💡 Are there any new questions you would like to ask about the map on page 186? Write these down.

Why was Cuba important?

Cuba is a small island near the southern tip of Florida, in the USA. In 1959 Cuba became communist and developed close links with the USSR. Nikita Khrushchev, the Soviet President, was pleased to be linked with a country so close to the USA. The USA already had missile launch sites on the USSR's border with Turkey. A missile launched from one of these sites could reach Moscow in five to ten minutes. The USSR felt threatened.

💡 Does this additional information help you to answer any of your questions from page 186? Use this to try to explain what you now think the map on page 186 is showing us.

The Cuban Missile Crisis – what happened?

The Cuban Missile Crisis was the most serious crisis in the Cold War period. It almost caused a nuclear war between the USA and the USSR. People around the world were very frightened of a nuclear war. The timeline below shows how the crisis developed and how it ended.

TIMELINE
The Cuban Missile Crisis, October 1962

Tuesday 16	Nuclear missile launch sites are photographed on Cuba by US spy planes. Missiles could hit most US cities within seventeen minutes. They would be ready to launch in seven days. At the same time, twenty ships from the USSR are seen heading towards Cuba carrying nuclear missiles. The US President, John Kennedy, has to decide what to do. There may already be nuclear missiles in Cuba.
Monday 22	President Kennedy uses his navy to blockade (surround) Cuba to prevent the Soviet ships from getting through.
Tuesday 23	President Khrushchev threatens to use his ships to break through the blockade if necessary. This would be an act of war.
Wednesday 24	The first Soviet ships approach the blockade zone. At 10.32 am, they stop and turn around.
Thursday 25	Some of President Kennedy's advisers tell him to invade Cuba and destroy the remaining missiles. This would be an act of war.
Friday 26	Khrushchev agrees to remove the missiles if Kennedy lifts the blockade and promises not to invade Cuba.
Saturday 27	Kennedy's advisers urge him to invade Cuba, despite Khrushchev's offer.
Sunday 28	Kennedy accepts Khrushchev's offer. He also agrees secretly to remove US missiles from Turkey. Russian missiles are removed from Cuba. The crisis is over.

A cartoon about the Cuban Missile Crisis, published in 1962. Kennedy is on the right; Khrushchev is on the left.

TASKS...

Look at the outline of a diary and the clockface. This is the Nuclear Clock. It was designed by the US magazine *Bulletin* in 1947. It was a symbol of nuclear danger. The time was set at seven minutes to midnight. Minutes were taken off or added on depending how close a nuclear war was thought to be. **WS**

Cuban Missile Crisis Diary

Tuesday 16

Monday 22

Tuesday 23

Wednesday 24

Thursday 25

Friday 26

Saturday 27

Sunday 28

1 Fill in the diary for each day of the Cuban Missile Crisis. Use the information on the timeline (page 188) for information. Follow these instructions.

- For each day in the diary, draw the Nuclear Clock. Decide how many minutes should be added or taken away. Then put the time on your clock.

- Add or take away one, two or three minutes each day. The number will depend on how dangerous you think the situation has become. If there is no change on one day then leave the clock at the same time as the previous day.

- If the clock reaches midnight then war has broken out.

- You need to explain in your diary entry why the events of the day have made you change the clock.

- Say how you will be feeling on each day of the crisis.

2 Look carefully at your completed diary. On which day were you closest to midnight? Explain why.

3 What time was it on your clock at the end of the crisis? What do you think this tells you about the way the crisis was ended?

Who 'won' the Cuban Missile Crisis?

Both the USA and the USSR claimed victory in the Cuban Missile Crisis. Look at what US President Kennedy and USSR President Khrushchev said about the end of the crisis.

I have proved that I can challenge the communist Soviet Union. I can force it to back down without causing a war. The USA is no longer threatened with nuclear attack from Cuba because of my firm but sensible approach.

President Kennedy.

I have stopped a nuclear war because I was prepared to negotiate. The Americans have gained nothing. Cuba is still communist. Kennedy has promised to remove his missiles from Turkey (though he will not admit this publicly).

President Khrushchev.

SOURCE B

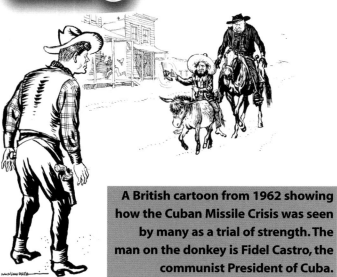

A British cartoon from 1962 showing how the Cuban Missile Crisis was seen by many as a trial of strength. The man on the donkey is Fidel Castro, the communist President of Cuba.

The Cold War was a war of threats and propaganda. Many cartoons like those shown in Sources A and B were published about the Cuban Missile Crisis, each giving its own view of events.

TASKS...

1 In pairs, design two propaganda posters about the end of the Cuban Missile Crisis. One poster will show the USA's attitude and the other the Soviet point of view. Think carefully about the words and pictures you are going to use to persuade people (you can use cartoons if you prefer).

2 Put all the posters on display. Have a class discussion about which is the most successful and why.

3 Look back at your comparison chart, which you started on page 179. Now add a third row about the Cuban Missile Crisis (as shown below), and complete the details for each aspect of warfare.

Conflict	Main weapons	Tactics used	Who won?
First World War: Battle of the Somme			
Second World War: the fall of France			
Cold war: the Cuban Missile Crisis			

EXTENSION TASK...

4 Use all of the information on your comparison chart and the information in this chapter to answer these questions. Use as much evidence as you can in your answers.
- Do you think that trench warfare in the First World War was a successful battle tactic?
- Does the German's use of *Blitzkrieg* mean that they were more advanced than other countries fighting in the Second World War?
- Why do you think that the Cold War remained only a war of words and propaganda?
- In modern warfare, did anyone really win?

Plenary

Having studied the Battle of the Somme during the First World War, the fall of the French during the Second World War and the Cuban Missile Crisis during the Cold War, which aspect of warfare do you think has changed:

a) the most   b) the least.

Discuss this with a partner and the rest of the class. How far do you agree with each other?

10 HAS THE IMPACT OF WAR ON CIVILIANS CHANGED DURING THE TWENTIETH CENTURY?

HOW WERE PEOPLE RECRUITED FOR THE FIRST AND SECOND WORLD WARS?

Objectives

In this section you will find out:
- attitudes towards recruitment at the start of the First World War and the Second World War, and during the Vietnam War
- whether these attitudes changed.

To investigate these ideas you will:
- study different propaganda posters.

Starter

SOURCE A

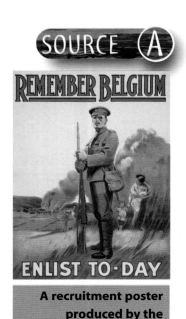

A recruitment poster produced by the government in 1915.

SOURCE B

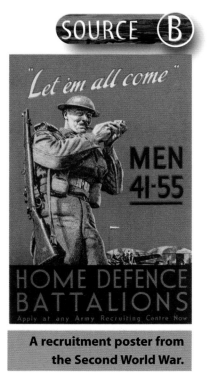

A recruitment poster from the Second World War.

SOURCE C

An American anti-war poster from the Vietnam war.

Look at Sources A, B and C on page 192.

💡 *How do these posters attract people's attention?*

💡 *What impression do they give of warfare?*

💡 *Which poster is the odd one out? Why?*

What happened at the start of the First World War?

The outbreak of war in 1914 was met with great excitement. Britain and Europe was soon in the grip of **war fever**. People were keen to show how **patriotic** they were and how much they hated the Germans.

Key words

War fever Enthusiasm for war.
Patriotic Love for and devotion to your country.
Enlist To sign up (join) the armed forces.

What an adventure! A chance to escape from the poor, grimy streets where I live and to see new places!

The war will be over by Christmas.

I don't want to miss the chance to fight with my friends for my King and Country.

Our town has more men fighting than any of the other towns nearby.

I'm a proud man. I won't let anyone down!

My friends and I, we'll all be fighting together.

A young working-class recruit in 1914.

At first there was great enthusiasm for the war. Even so, the government thought there would not be enough soldiers to fight. So a huge poster campaign began to encourage men to volunteer to become soldiers. After a month, half a million men had **enlisted**. By 1916, the number had reached two million.

Why the government introduced conscription in 1916

In the first two years of the war, casualties were very high. Fewer men volunteered to fight as they heard about the terrible conditions in the trenches. So, in 1916, the government ordered that all men between 18 and 40 years of age 'join up'. This was called conscription.

Conscientious objectors ('Conchies')

Conscientious objectors were those men who refused to join the army. Many refused because they did not agree with fighting and killing. 'Conchies' were very unpopular – people said that they were cowards. They had to appear before Military Tribunal Officers (a military court) to explain their reasons for not fighting. Some of these reasons are shown below.

> Conscription is wrong. Men should be free to decide for themselves if they want to fight.

> I do love my country but war is wrong. I refuse to kill other human beings.

> I am a Quaker by religion. I believe in non-violence.

> My job is needed to fight the war. So I should stay at home and work. I don't believe in this war. It's wrong!

> My sight and health are poor. What use would I be in the army?

TASKS...

1   Look at the reasons in the speech bubbles that the conscientious objectors give for not wanting to fight. Divide them into two lists – those that the Military Tribunal Officers will sympathise with, and those they will refuse to accept. Explain your choices to other pupils.

2   Look back to Sources A to C, which show propaganda posters used by the British government during the First World War to recruit soldiers. What words and images do they use to persuade men to enlist?

3   Design a poster for conscientious objectors to spread their beliefs about war and violence.
    Remember: you have to show that they were patriotic even though they did not believe in fighting. Think about the words and images you will need to use to show this.

What happened during the Second World War?

On 3 September 1939, Britain declared war on Germany. All men between the ages of eighteen and 40 were conscripted into the army. Only coal miners, firemen and doctors were **exempt**.

- 💡 *Why do you think that soldiers were conscripted as soon as war started in 1939?*

- 💡 *What lessons do you think the government had learnt from the First World War?*

- 💡 *Why do you think the three groups of men mentioned above were exempt?*

How had conscription changed since the First World War?

SOURCE D

A poster from the Second World War advertising for women to help the war effort by working in factories.

The outbreak of the Second World War excited some people as it had done in 1914. However, to most people, war was no longer attractive. After the First World War, they knew that war brought sorrow, death and destruction.

This time the government had to make sure that people supported the war, so it passed the Emergency Powers Defence Act. This meant that everyone in Britain had to follow government orders. The Act gave the government the power to take over any property that was needed for the war. There was also a huge propaganda campaign asking everyone to do his or her bit to help.

As a result of conscription, more than one million men had joined the army by 1940. On the **home front**, the people of Britain also responded well to the government's request for support.

> ### Key words
>
> **Exempt** Free from duty.
> **Home front** The people defending the country and contributing to the war effort 'at home' in Britain.

A poster encouraging men to volunteer for the Home Guard ('Dad's Army'). These were unpaid, part-time volunteers who were too old for military service. They were trained to defend Britain against invasion.

All the fighting nations are involved, not only soldiers, but the whole population – men, women and children. Every town, village and street is defended. Every road is guarded. Factories are working for the war. The workmen are soldiers with different weapons, but the same courage.

Spoken by Winston Churchill, the British prime minister, in 1940.

TASKS...

1 Suppose you had done nothing so far to help the war effort. Then you hear Churchill's speech (Source F). How would it make you feel? Try to explain what you would feel and why.

2 What could children and young people have done to help the war effort?

3 If you owned some land, you could probably have made some money for yourself, growing vegetables and selling them, for example. So how would you have felt if the government informed you it was taking your land? Explain your answer.

4 Try to find out what men, women and children did during the Second World War in your local area. (For example, you could interview local people you know.)

THE VIETNAM WAR

After 1945, the USA and the Soviet Union became 'superpowers' (the most powerful countries). Each one had different ideas about how a country and its people should be governed. Each was suspicious of the other.

In 1954, North Vietnam became communist. The North Vietnamese wanted to unite North and South Vietnam under one communist government. The USA was afraid that if one country in the Far East became communist, all those around it would soon follow (the 'domino theory'). The USA wanted to stop this happening.

So in 1964, the Vietnam War began. At first, the American people agreed that the government had to stop the spread of communism. But by 1970, public opinion in the USA was changing dramatically because:

- US casualties were very high. The tactics of the North Vietnamese (Vietcong) were hard to fight

- by 1969, half a million US troops were fighting in Vietnam but there seemed no end to the war in sight.

So the American people began to oppose the war. Anti-war demonstrations took place. They wanted their young men home.

TASKS...

Look at the spider diagram on page 198. Using the spider diagram and the information on this page, answer the following questions.

1 Why did so many people object to the war in Vietnam?

2 Which of the different groups that opposed the Vietnam War do you think had the greatest impact on public opinion? Give reasons for your answers.

3 Draw an arrow like the one on page 179. Give examples of six words which you think people would have most and least commonly used during the Vietnam War

'No' say the general public

The American people soon became unhappy with their government's involvement in the Vietnam War. The war was televised and people were horrified to see young US soldiers commit terrible atrocities. Even worse, the number of soldiers brought home in body bags increased.

YOU WILL FIGHT!

'No' say the war veterans

Veterans (ex-soldiers) of the Vietnam War made stirring speeches about the horror of the war. Many of these had been badly injured and crippled. They threw their war medals into the crowd.

'No' say the students

Young men burnt their draft cards (a call-up card) in public places. Some students left the country to avoid having to fight; others formed a 'We Won't Go' group. By 1969, around 34,000 young men were avoiding the draft.

Plenary

In March 2003, thousands of people took to the streets in mass demonstrations across the world in order to show their disapproval of the war against Iraq.

- 💡 Why do you think so many people in the twenty-first century disapprove of war?

- 💡 Are any of your reasons linked to experiences of the First World War, Second World War or Vietnam War?

EVERYDAY LIFE: WHAT IMPACT DOES WARFARE HAVE ON CIVILIANS?

Objectives

In this section you will find out:
- how the impact of warfare on civilians' lives varied greatly during the First and Second World Wars and the Vietnam War
- how the government introduced laws to influence civilians' everyday lives
- the differences between short-term and long-term effects of warfare on civilian lives.

To investigate these ideas you will:
- categorise the ways in which civilians were affected.

Starter

How do you think you would feel if a foreign power invaded Britain?

How do you think that your everyday life would change?

Would you try to resist? What methods would you use?

Write down your thoughts about these questions and share them with others in the class.

What were civilians' experiences during the First World War?

Read the conversation between Joan and Doris on page 200 and then look at Sources A, B and C on page 201.

A conversation between Doris and Joan in 1918

Oh, Doris! Can you believe, how much our lives have changed since war began?

I know. The country went mad with excitement. It's hard to believe it was just three years ago. Will it ever end?

Our lives have changed, haven't they? It's strange with all the men away fighting. Then there's all those who have been killed. I can't think about it without feeling sad and angry. They're obviously running out of soldiers fast! It's not suprising that men aren't volunteering anymore.

Ever since the Defence of the Realm Act (see page 201, Source A) was passed in 1914, the government seems to have completely taken over our lives!

Yes, we can't even talk about where our husbands are without risking getting into trouble. Mind you, we don't really know where they are. All our letters are censored. We only know what the government wants us to know. The radio and newspapers are censored too.

Can you remember the last time you went flying kites with the children? Or stood beside bonfires and watched fireworks? I really miss the church bells on Sunday mornings.

Chance would be a fine thing! All the open spaces are being used for growing crops now. The government even tells you where you can and cannot walk. Allotments and railway lines are out of bounds.

Mind you, we don't do too badly. We're fairly safe, we have enough food and we don't see many Zeppelin air raids, do we?

It makes sense to grow our own food. Those German U-boats are stopping food coming from abroad. They're trying to starve us into giving up. I agree with rationing. It's only fair to share things out. That way, everyone gets some sugar, margarine and meat, even though it's not much.

The older men miss their social life – especially drinking! They complain that the beer has been watered down so they don't like drinking it.

Oh well, no more time for talking. Its nearly time for my shift to start at the munitions factory.

At least when the war is over our lives can get back to normal!

The government passed the Defence of the Realm Act (DORA) in August 1914. Never before had the government had so much power over people's lives.

- People could be told where to work.
- Railways and coal mines were taken over by the government.
- British Summer Time was introduced – clocks went forward to give an extra hour of daylight.

- In 1916, bank holidays were cancelled. So was Bonfire night!
- Pub opening hours were cut and beer was watered down.
- People could not buy a friend a drink or give bread to an animal.
- Newspapers were censored (they were only able to print what the government allowed them to).

A modern historian describes the effects of DORA.

SOURCE B

SOURCE C

A government poster of 1917.

A government poster of 1917 encouraging women to join the Women's Land Army.

- Make a list of the changes that Doris and Joan talk about on page 200.

- Look at Sources A, B and C. Then look again at the list of changes in Doris and Joan's conversation. At the side of each point on your list write the letter of the source that supports it.

TASKS...

1 Look at the conversation between Doris and Joan, and Sources A, B and C.

a) Copy and complete the chart below in order to show as many changes as possible to civilian lifestyles. (You should give at least five changes.)

b) For each change, say why you think it was introduced.

Change introduced by DORA	Why it was introduced	Impact on civilian lives (number 1–5)	Reason for decision

c) Next, choose three colours.
- Use one colour to shade the big changes to people's lives.
- Use another colour to shade those changes that had some effect on people's lives.
- Use the third colour to shade those changes that had no effect on people's lives.

d) In the last column, write down your reasons for your decisions.

2 Do you think that the First World War had a huge effect on the everyday lives of civilians? Discuss your reasons with a partner.

3 What other information would help you to understand more about the full effects of the First World War on civilians' everyday life?

How did life change for civilians during the Second World War?

Life on the Home Front during the Second World War

- People put paper and metal into collection bins to help the war effort. Paper could be recycled; bones were used to make gun cartridges; Spitfire planes were made from aluminium pans and iron railings.

- Street names and signposts were taken down so that invaders could not find their way around.

- Gas masks were issued to everyone at the outbreak of war. Plans were also made to evacuate children from the towns to the safety of the countryside.

- From January 1940, every family had a ration book. Everybody was allowed to buy a small amount of meat, sugar, tea, coffee and tobacco (see Source F). They could only buy their rations from one shop.

- Food shortages resulted from the sinking of ships carrying food and supplies to Britain, so people were encouraged to grow their own food.

- Many people grew fruit and vegetables in their gardens and allotments, because this food was not rationed. They also kept hens and geese.

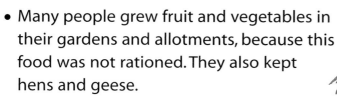

A public information leaflet telling people what to do to protect themselves against gas attacks.

People were told by the government to 'Make Do and Mend'. Old woollens were undone and re-knitted into warm clothing for British troops. Nylon parachute material was sold for underwear. Sheets were patched or turned into bandages. Envelopes were re-used and newspapers were recycled. Food scraps were collected in bins on street corners to feed pigs.

A modern historian writing in 2002.

A pamphlet supplied by the Ministry of Food in 1941, describing how to use rations effectively.

Milk	6 glasses
Eggs	1 per fortnight
Meat	500 grams
Butter or magarine	300 grams
Sugar	2 teacups
Cooking oil	$\frac{1}{2}$ a teacup
Tea	just under 1 teacup of dry tea leaves
Cheese	225 grams
Jam	$1\frac{1}{2}$ teacups

Average weekly adult ration during wartime.

SOURCE H

SOURCE I

Government posters encouraged people to join the war effort. They could work hard and save. Posters warned people not to talk carelessly about the war in public places. They could be giving information to a spy!

From a modern textbook.

Fishermen on Holy Island, off the north-east coast of England, learning to use rifles as part of their Home Guard training

- The country was defended against invasion by the Home Guard. These soldiers were too young, too old or unfit to fight. Some were First World War veterans.
- Anderson Shelters were built in houses with gardens. These were made from steel sheets and buried 4ft deep.
- People were ordered to put up blackout curtains. These stopped any light escaping that might guide enemy bomber planes. They were checked by Air Raid Wardens.

TASKS...

1 Read the information on pages 202–4 and Sources D to I on the impact of war on civilians' lives during Second World War. **a)** Draw a larger copy of this chart into your books.

Changes to protect the population during an air raid.

Changes to protect the population in the event of an invasion.

Examples of changes that were made.

Changes that contribute to the war effort and make life easier.

b) Find examples from your reading to include in the three boxes.

TASKS...

2 Look back to the conversation between Doris and Joan talking about the First World War on page 200.

With a partner, re-write the conversation between Doris and Joan. This time, their conversation should be about how life changed in the Second World War and why these changes occurred.

3 Which war do you think affected people the most? Why? Have a class discussion about this.

How did the Blitz affect life in Britain?

During the Second World War, both the German and British governments bombed industrial and military targets as well as railways. Both governments wanted to cause large numbers of civilian casualties. They hoped that the constant fear of bombing raids would break the people's support for the war. Then they would demand that the government make peace or even surrender. This had happened in Germany at the end of the First World War. People were starving there because German ports were blockaded by enemy ships. No food could enter Germany. So they put pressure on the government to end the war.

SOURCE J

7 October 1940	We must continue to attack England on all fronts.
11 October 1940	We shall be able to force England to its knees during the next few weeks.
12 October 1940	Horrific reports from London. A city on the point of destruction. We must keep up the pressure.
23 October 1940	We shall battle on to destroy their last hope.
1 November 1940	Hitler intends to keep hammering the English until they break.

Extracts from the diary of Joseph Goebbels, one of the most senior Nazis, during intense bombing raids on Britain.

SOURCE K

We will make the enemy burn and bleed in every way.

A quote from Winston Churchill in 1941.

💡 Make a list of the words and phrases in Sources B and C that tell you the reasons for the British and German bombing raids during the Second World War?

SOURCE L

Coventry Cathedral in ruins after a night of heavy bombing during the Blitz, November 1940. The city centre was destroyed and over 500 people were killed.

What happened in the Blitz?

Between autumn 1940 and May 1941, the Germans repeatedly bombed London, Coventry, Manchester, and many other industrial and coastal areas. These attacks became known as the Blitz. Thousands of houses were destroyed and thousands of civilians were injured and killed, despite attempts to protect them (see Sources H and I on page 207).

The government issued everyone with gas masks in case of gas attacks. Children were evacuated to safety in the countryside. Even so, casualty rates during the Blitz were huge.

By May 1941, more than 43,000 people across Britain had been killed. Even more were homeless. At this point in the war, more British women and children had been killed than soldiers.

SOURCE M

Children from London evacuated to the Sussex coast, awaiting transport to their new homes, July 1940.

SOURCE N

Schoolchildren	827,000
Mothers and children	524,000
Pregnant women	13,000
Blind and disabled people	7000
Teachers	103,000

Number of people evacuated in September 1939.

The church was a popular shelter so it was full when the bomb fell. Mostly women and children were hit when it exploded. It looked like a massacre. Bodies, limbs and flesh were mixed with little hats, coats and shoes. The worst thing was knowing that these horrible pieces of flesh had once been living, breathing people.

An account of the Blitz from a fireman, September 1940.

People sleeping in a Morrison (air raid) shelter, set up in their living room in London, September 1940.

Morrison shelters proved their worth over and over again. These could be buried in debris yet the families came out of them uninjured and smiling. Their homes had been destroyed around them but they had been kept safe by the shelter.

From an Exeter newspaper in May 1942. Exeter was very badly hit by bombs during the war.

The story of the last weekend is one of panic. The newspaper stories telling of life going on as usual are untrue. There was no bread, no milk and no telephones. There is no humour or laughter.

From a report by local officials on conditions in London, September 1940.

A photograph, posed for propaganda purposes, showing a milkman delivering among the ruins of a bombed city.

HAS THE IMPACT OF WAR ON CIVILIANS CHANGED?

Extensive bomb damage in Walthamstow, London, September 1944.

TASKS...

1 **a)** Look at Sources K to T. Write down five words that describe how British civilians might have felt during the Blitz.

   b) In pairs, share your words. Pick out the ones that are different. Expain to each other why you chose these words.

2 Look at Sources K, L, O, Q and T.

   a) If you were the editor of a British newspaper during the Second World War, which pictures would you use? Why?

   b) Which pictures would a German newspaper editor use? Why?

   c) Write a bold headline that might appear in either a German or a British newspaper to go with your pictures.

3 Look at Sources K, L, O, Q and T. If you had to write about what really happened in the Blitz, what other things would you want to know? Where might you find the answers?

What impact did warfare have on civilians during the Vietnam War?

The original napalm bomb wasn't so hot. If the **gooks** were quick, they could scrape it off. So the boys added polystyrene which sticks. But it stopped burning if they jumped into water. So they added white phosphorous, to make it burn better. Phosphorous burns under water. One drop is enough. It burns right down to the bone.

A US pilot describes the effects of bombing with napalm.

Key words

Gooks A slang term that US soldiers used to refer to the Vietnamese.

The story below is based on real events from the Vietnam War.

I was lucky to survive. Many of my family, friends and fellow villagers died when our land was attacked. The sights that I saw were horrifying. People being shot at point blank range, women abused, whole villages and crops burned.

Over four million Vietnamese people were killed during this war. Booby traps left in the countryside and rice fields have killed many since. Over 25,000 square kilometres of forest were destroyed by both US and Vietcong soldiers.

Many people were horribly disfigured by napalm burns. Some were so disfigured that they hid themselves away from other people in shame.

The beautiful countryside of Vietnam was destroyed by the chemical, Agent Orange. The landscape remains scarred today by huge craters left by the B52 bombers [US planes carrying Agent Orange]. People can be seen today fishing in them.

SOURCE (V)

SOURCE (W)

Dead civilians, massacred at My Lai by US soldiers, 1968.

Vietnamese children flee after a napalm attack , 1972.

HAS THE IMPACT OF WAR ON CIVILIANS CHANGED?

At the time, Agent Orange attacks caused many Vietnamese people to suffer from sickness and headaches. Babies are still born deformed, and people still suffer from cancers as a result of Agent Orange, which poisoned our water supplies.

I was lucky. I managed to escape before the North Vietnamese soldiers took over South Vietnam in 1975. There were thousands of us with nowhere to go. But we had to escape. We were afraid of what would happen if we stayed.

For those who stayed, life was hard. There were so many orphans and injured civilians. There was high unemployment. People were starving, because the crop fields had been destroyed. The USA also stopped countries trading with us.

Some people tried to leave Vietnam illegally. They went by boat so they became known as the Boat People. All they wanted was a place to be safe. However, few survived. If they survived pirate attacks on their boats, they were refused entry to the countries they hoped would give them refuge.

What a mess the Vietnam War left us all in!

TASKS...

1 **a)** According to Source U, what impact did the Vietnam War have on civilians' everyday life?

   b) What other questions would you like to ask to find out more about the effect of the Vietnam War on civilians' lives?

2 Copy this diagram (right) into your books. On it you are going to write examples of:

   a) the short-term effects of the Vietnam War on civilians' everyday lives

   b) the long-term effects of the Vietnam War on civilians' everyday lives.

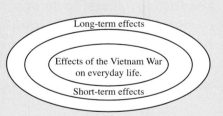

Long-term effects

Effects of the Vietnam War on everyday life.

Short-term effects

3 What links can you make between any of the short-term and long-term effects of the Vietnam War on civilians' everyday lives? Draw arrows on your diagram to show these.

Plenary

Write down three ways in which the effects of the Vietnam War on civilians' everyday lives were the same as those of the First and Second World Wars.

Write down five ways in which the effects were different.

WHAT IMPACT HAS WAR HAD ON WOMEN'S LIVES?

Objectives

In this section you will find out:
- why women's roles changed during the First World War and the Second World War
- what impact these changes had on the position of women in society.

To investigate these ideas you will:
- analyse the work that women did
- evaluate a variety of sources.

Starter

Our industries are suffering. We are not making enough ammunition for our soldiers on the **Western Front**.

Urgent help is needed for injured soldiers on the battlefield.

There are too many men doing clerical jobs; they are needed for fighting.

Not enough food is arriving in Britain. How much longer can we feed our people?

Life may become chaotic – there are no men left to do the work at home.

💡 These were the problems that faced a government minister during the First World War. Which do you think is most serious? Why?

💡 What suggestions would you make to the government minister to solve some of the problems?

Key words

Western Front The area in France and Belgium where the Allied forces were fighting the Germans.

What was the impact of the First World War on women?

When the First World War broke out in 1914, about 190,000 women workers lost their jobs. These women worked mainly in the textiles industry or were domestic servants – no one wanted to buy new clothes in wartime or employ help with their families.

By 1915, more ammunition was needed for soldiers on the Western Front, so women were given the jobs that men had done before they went to fight. It was agreed that the women could have these jobs until the men returned from war. However, the women were not given the same pay as the men!

A Women's War Register was set up to find out which women were available for war work. The register had a fantastic response. After two weeks, about 33,000 women had signed up. This rose to more than 100,000 women in the next few months.

However, by 1916, so many men were fighting abroad that there was a serious shortage of workers at home – there were about two million vacancies. Something had to be done quickly, so a government propaganda campaign encouraged women to help through either voluntary organisations or paid employment. Women began to work where they had never worked before.

Organisations women joined during the First World War

- **Voluntary Aid Detachment (VADs)**
Volunteer nurses, working on the Western Front, helping injured soldiers.

- **Women's Auxiliary Corps (WAAC)**
Women's army unit. They did the clerical work in the army. The men they replaced were able to fight. They also worked as army cooks and drivers.

- **Women's Royal Naval Service (WRNS) and Women's Royal Air force (WRAF)**
These organisations were like the WAAC, but they worked for the Navy and Air Force instead.

- **Women's Land Army**
Women who worked on the farms, cultivating the land and growing crops and food. They became known as Land Girls.

SOURCE A

What will you tell your children about what you did in the First World War? I wanted to serve my country. I was also thrilled by the adventure of doing things that were completely new to me. I was going to put myself to the test to discover if I was fit to serve my country. My work would involve handling a machine, and I was afraid of machinery.

Monica Cosens, who worked in a munitions factory during the First World War.

SOURCE B

Women working in a munitions factory in May 1917. They are doing skilled precision machine work.

SOURCE C

We went on duty at 7.30 am and came off at 8 pm, including three hours off and a weekly half day.

Vera Brittain, a nurse in France during the First World War.

SOURCE D

Women air mechanics of the Women's Royal Air Force (WRAF), established in 1918.

SOURCE E

The work women are doing is not monotonous. It demands very little physical skill. It challenges the intelligence of the workers. Even so, the work produced is excellent.

From a trade journal, *The Engineer*, 20 August 1915.

SOURCE F

The first dressing I assisted was to an infected leg wound, slimy and green and scarlet with the bone laid bare. It turned me sick and faint for a moment.

Vera Brittain writing about her experiences as a nurse during the First World War.

Land girls on a farm in Surrey, April 1917.

London has not yet got used to its policewomen. I saw one today at the corner of Whitehall. She appeared self-conscious. These women are not really built to face the hurly-burly of a street fight.

A report from a newspaper report of May 1915, describing public reactions to women members of the police force.

TASKS...

1 Look back to the problems that the government minister faced during the First World War (page 211). Copy the chart below to show how women helped to solve each problem.

Problem	How women helped with the war effort	Skills required
How to help the injured soldiers on the battlefield.		
How to free men from clerical jobs so they can fight.		
How to provide more food for the British people.		
How to provide more munitions on the Western Front.		
How to keep life on the Home Front as organised and calm as possible.		

2 What do you think was the most important job women did to contribute to the war effort? Give reasons for your answer.

What was the impact of the Second World War on women?

Throughout the Second World War, British civilians were in constant danger from air raids, invasion and food shortages. Women were expected to keep things going at home, as they had done during the First World War.

Government ministers stressed the importance of women's role as the main line of defence on the Home Front. Once again, a government propaganda campaign attracted women to volunteer for work. It was made to look glamorous.

SOURCE I

Women working in a gas mask factory during the Second World War.

SOURCE J

SOURCE K

Working in factories is not fun. It was grim being shut in for hours on end without even a window to see daylight. The noise was terrific. At night, when you tried to sleep, the noise was still there in your head. Night shifts were the worst. The work was very often monotonous and it was boring.

One woman describes her experiences of working in a factory in 1942.

A friend of mine was caught in the blast from a bomb and was taken to hospital with several shrapnel wounds. The all-clear [a signal to say that the enemy attack was over] went at about 6 am and we went home to bed. Two hours later, I got up and went to work.

Doreen Ellis, writing in her diary about life during the Second World War.

SOURCE L

The men were lying in various positions. Often their limbs stuck out at queer angles in the plaster splints or sometimes they were slung on frames and hung with weights and pulleys. The light caught the glass flasks of blood, which was still slowly dripping into four bed cases.

Lena K. Chivers, a nurse at a casualty clearing station, August 1944.

SOURCE M

When I went shopping for my mother, it sometimes took a whole morning even though the shops were just round the corner. Most of the time was spent queuing – especially for bread and meat. My mother and her friends queued for hours.

A woman recalls how rationing affected her family during the war.

SOURCE N

Women servicing a six-ton truck during the Second World War.

SOURCE O

A poster calling for women to join the Women's Land Army.

SOURCE P

My white tender hands were gone. Instead, they became rough and hard. When I rolled into bed at the end of the day, I laid still not daring to move in case the pounding backache moved all around my aching body.

A woman called Ivy, talking about life in the Land Army.

SOURCE Q

We worked for twelve hours a day on a farm in Lincolnshire. The work was hard and boring. There was no training. Wages were 28 shillings (£1.40) a week. We had to pay £1 for our lodgings. At a smaller farm in Huntingdon, instead of being trained in tractor driving, we had to do odd jobs. This included kitchen work for the farmer's wife. He gave us no training and refused to pay us any wages.

One woman's description of her work as a Land Girl in 1941.

SOURCE R

British women often give orders to men. The men obey smartly and are not ashamed. For British women have proved themselves in this war. They have stuck to their posts near burning ammunition dumps. They have delivered messages on foot after their motorcycles have been blown from under them. They have pulled pilots from burning planes. They have died at their gun-posts and quickly been replaced by another girl. No British woman in uniformed service has quit her post or failed in her duty under fire. When you see a girl in uniform wearing a medal, remember that she didn't get it for knitting more socks than anyone else.

An extract from a booklet issued by the US War Department to every US soldier entering Britain during the war.

TASKS...

1   Copy and complete the chart below.

Sources which glamorise women's work	Sources which show the reality of women's work

Now place the letter of Sources I to R in the correct column, to show which ones glamorise women's work and which show the reality.

2   Take two examples from each column of your chart. Explain how each example either glamorises women's work or shows what it was really like.

3   Choose either the 'Glamorising images' or 'Reality images' column of your chart. Now write a speech from the point of view of the women involved in those images about:
  • food shortages   • threats of invasion   • damage caused by air raids.
  Remember, you need to be either very positive or negative in your approach, depending on which sources you are using.

4 You are now in a position to judge how warfare changed the position of British women in the twentieth century. Copy the diagram below into your book. You should write down key points about women's role during both the First and Second World Wars on your diagram.

- Any similarities between women's roles should be written down in the overlapping section of the two circles.
- The differences should be listed in the correct circle.

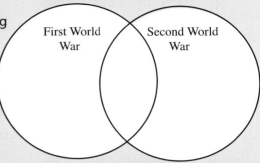

First World War

Second World War

5 Read the statements below.

- The First and Second World Wars have made no impact at all on women's lives.
- The First World War made a small impact on women's lives, but it was not until the Second World War that women's lives really changed.
- Both wars made a huge lasting impact on women's lives.

Which view do you support? Explain your decision.

Plenary

 SOURCE S

 SOURCE T

Nature doth show women to be weak, frail, impatient, feeble and foolish. For a woman to rule over a kingdom, nation or city is against to nature and God's revealed will.

John Knox, a sixteenth-century Scottish preacher.

Modern British female soldier.

💡 Do you think that women and men in the twenty-first century would agree with John Knox's comment (Source S)? Explain your thoughts.

Do you know of any places in the world where women today are still treated as second-class citizens? Give some examples. Why do you think women are still treated in this way in these places?

THE CHANGING NATURE OF WARFARE IN THE TWENTIETH CENTURY: CONCLUSION

A local museum is planning an exhibition with the title 'The changing nature of warfare in the twentieth century'. You have been asked to suggest six exhibits. These can be photographs, paintings, drawings, artefacts (objects) and written sources.

For each exhibit, you must provide a commentary explaining why it is important that it is included. Remember – each exhibit must show visitors about the way warfare changed.

Your exhibits must cover all the twentieth century, not just one war.

Complete this exercise on a larger copy of this exhibit sheet:

Exhibit	Why should it be included in the exhibition?	Explain what the exhibit shows and why it is important in explaining the changing nature of warfare in the twentieth century.

Index